WINE & SPIRIT

A Christian's Guide to Enjoying Wine

Jerry Butler

Published by L'Edge Press
A ministry of Upside Down Ministries, Inc.
PO Box 2567
Boone, NC 28607

Graphic Design by Abbie Frease
www.abbiefrease.com

To Sherry
With love and gratitude

CONTENTS

FOREWORD

Although a native wine-drinking Frenchman, I was employed since the mid-sixties in an evangelical but non-fundamentalist American educational institution that required all of its constituency, from top-level board members to incoming freshmen to subscribe to a life-style code of conduct that was commonly called the "pledge." For more than a century, this requirement contained an article that prohibited all signatories to own or to use alcoholic beverages either on or off campus.

When I became acquainted with this prohibition during my first interview, I protested that, neither on the basis of conviction nor of practice, I could adhere to it. I explained how, from the age of thirteen, my family had introduced me to drinking a tiny amount of wine diluted with water at evening meals and how the amount was increased every year until I could have a full glass when I attained maturity. I assured my interlocutors that wine was a dietary element of my food intake and that I did not drink outside of meals. I self-righteously but truthfully added that I had never been drunk in my life.

My argument cut no ice. I was told that the prohibition was absolute and that it was based on prudential as well as biblical considerations. I finally signed the pledge after I was advised to place my call to teach ahead of carnal desires, being assured that I would gain victory over my sinful propensity if I made it a matter of prayer.

Unfortunately, things did not work that way. After a few weeks of abstinence, I developed digestive problems and went to the dean's office to inform him that the victory was not happening. With a twinkle in his eye, the gentleman advised me to go see Dr. Paul Parker for a treatment. Without even checking my insides, the good doctor made a quick diagnosis of my condition and wrote a prescription "for my stomach's sake."

With the use of all necessary discretion, the physician's prescription helped me survive for decades in that environment. Deliverance from my illicit medical gratification came only after my retirement, when the prohibition against drinking was abrogated for the whole campus except for persons under legal age. To this day, a group of grateful connoisseurs holds a party every year on the date of the change of policy to celebrate adequately accession from legalistic bondage to freedom in Christ.

The book you hold in your hands vibrates with the same celebratory passion. Its author and I have been close friends for three decades. We have been involved together in many ministry ventures stateside and overseas. I don't remember us having had a bad day together except when we had to deal with culturally-benighted and spiritually-callow Christian leaders. The value of this book will be lost on such people. However, if you are a thankful believer, desirous to lead a life of praise and radiant witness, you will find much encouragement in the following pages. They may even guide you into the discovery of a new dimension of God's blessings available to us on earth with the promise of its renewal in eternity.

Gilbert Bilezikian
Professor Emeritus of Biblical Studies
Wheaton College

PREFACE

My early spiritual journey took me to a church with wonderful, loving people. I loved it, but my hunger to learn the truths of the Bible was perhaps a bit too strong, and I questioned everything. I also gave up drinking wine, as I was told by the Pastor that Christians do not drink. This put me off some, but I wanted to live the Christian life to the fullest, so I gave up wine for about a year, until I was invited to the neighbors to meet their new Pastor!

The new pastor, Bo, had a Bible that I thought was like a coloring book. It was multi-colored, front to back, with highlights detailing every subject line imaginable! I shared my story with Bo including my confusion about why Christians could not drink alcohol. We went through the Bible, cover to cover, detailing what the Bible really teaches about wine, strong drink, vineyards and our relationship with Him through this gift.

Later, I felt that God was compelling me to work in the wine industry, leading the way and opening doors to do so. Thirty years ago my wife and I moved to the Yakima Valley in Washington State and planted our vineyard at a time when there were only 13 wineries in the State. Now there are almost 700. God has blessed us with good wine, a beautiful vineyard, a successful business, and two of our three sons are trained winemakers, who are taking over the business.

I met Jerry Butler some 15 years ago in our winery's tasting room, and during our conversation about the wines I discovered that Jerry was an international pastor at a large Illinois church. Our conversation shifted from wine to the Church, and how conflicted the Church and Christians were on the subject of wine and alcohol in general. I am sure that Jerry was shocked to find a Christian winemaker as well!

Jerry shared that he was considering writing a book on the subject that would give an accurate perspective on the subject of wine from an historical, biblical and scientific basis, and I agreed to be a consultant from "the winemaker's" viewpoint. Over the years I had been given books and literature by Christians, that made well intentioned, but erroneous arguments and statements, attempting to prove that Christians should never drink alcohol—and especially arguing that wine mentioned in the Bible was really grape juice.

I am thankful and happy that Jerry Butler has written such a compelling book on wine and its relation to us through the Bible, science, and history. This book should be required reading for all Christians whether they drink or not.

Paul Portteus
Portteus Vineyards and Winery
Zillah, Washington

CHAPTER 1

UNCORKING CHRISTIANITY

I enjoy wine. So much so, I study it. I'm a "Christian." That is, I seek to model my life on the teachings and sayings of Jesus. What is wrong with this picture? Nothing! That's what's so great!

Standing at the site of Jesus' first miracle in Cana, one of my most memorable Sunday School classes came to mind. When I was fourteen, my Sunday school teacher was lecturing about Jesus turning water into wine at the wedding feast at Cana.

> On the third day, a wedding took place at Cana in Galilee.... Jesus said to the servants, "Fill the jars with water;" so they filled them to the brim. Then he told them, "Now draw some out and take it to the master of the banquet." They did so and the master of the banquet tasted the water that had been turned into wine. He did not realize where it had come from, though the servants who had drawn the water knew. Then he called the bridegroom aside and said, "Everyone brings out the choice wine first and then the cheaper wine after the guests have had too much to drink; but you have saved the best till now." (John 2: 1, 7-10)

After the reading, the teacher declared with emotion, "Your Jesus may have made wine, but mine didn't." "But it says he made wine," I responded. That didn't go over well at all. The teacher repeated that his Jesus didn't make wine. I thought,

"What's the big deal? It seems to me that my Jesus made wine!" The seed of a journey was planted.

Growing up in a conservative church in the South instilled a healthy dose of fear—fear about everything, but fear of drinking wine or any alcoholic beverage topped the list. "Drink wine and you will be kicked out of the church. Drink wine and you will go to hell."

Along with fear, we learned to be against everything that might give enjoyment, too much lightheartedness, or laughter and fun. After all, we were Christians. Being against things is what we did. I would later realize we acted out our fear with a strong dose of false piety and paranoia, and a sense of our "rightness" about everything.

My adventure into wine is an unexpected journey considering that I grew up in a conservative Christian home, and in a very conservative church in a very conservative dry county in the South.

The seed planted in that Sunday School class took root years later. I was living in the lush-green Oregon Willamette Valley. The valley is tucked between the blue-silhouetted Cascade Mountains to the east dominated by Mt. Hood, and the mountains of the Coast Range to the west. I happened to live in the valley in the emerging era of Oregon Pinot Noir. It was a great time to live in the Willamette Valley. There, wine forever secured a place in my life.

Living there provided my first lab for the study and appreciation of wine. I knew about wine—that wine is mentioned throughout the Bible, and that Jesus' first miracle was turning water into wine! Did you know that the Bible even gives directions on how to plant a vineyard? So the vineyards and wineries of the Willamette Valley, and the Bible morphed into a dual classroom for understanding wine. For over fifteen years I traversed the Valley visiting vineyards and wineries talking to winemakers about their craft, and picking up on their passion for wine. I turned the pages of the Bible finding an abundance of information and insight about wine. The connection to wine enlivened my spirit, my spiritual formation, and my growth as a human being.

Wine became a subject for spiritual and theological reflection. A tutor to life, as well as a drink to enjoy. Can wine really be all of that? With thirty years added to the journey, my answer is a passionate "Yes!"

Wine is a frequent metaphor in the Bible, teaching us about living in Spirit—living a life Jesus modeled for us. Then comes a great discovery: wine is a gift from God for our enjoyment. Arduous arguments are put forward claiming that wine in the Bible is grape juice. The other argument is that the Bible teaches abstinence, if not prohibition. The Bible speaks of wine on its own terms. All we will do is listen. In later chapters we'll do just that, as we look at the rich depository of wine-knowledge in the Bible.

Wine is a part of my table, as a complement to life, good food, and good times with friends and family. Wine is a beverage to enjoy. Wine also gives the gift of health. Wine offers many health benefits with daily, moderate drinking.

The past is the past, but sometime memories bring a smile, when we look back.

The county where I grew up was dry, meaning it was illegal to sell alcoholic beverages of any kind, anywhere. You would have to travel to a wet county to purchase beer, wine, and spirits. That was soon to change.

One Sunday our pastor announced, "We are going to war! The end times are coming to our town and county, and if we don't take to the streets and take a stand, we are doomed!" A ballot issue would give the citizens an opportunity to vote in favor of legalizing the sale of wine and beer in our county! I can still hear the gasps of the congregation. Now, I am not sure if it was genuine shock that our county might be on the slippery slope to doom, or a "slip" of excitement that they might not have to drive so far to stock up, but on any scale, this was big. The church lost the battle. The sale of wine and beer passed.

It didn't end there. The church added to the membership covenant that members were not to go into stores that sold alcoholic beverages. That worked for awhile. Soon, it was hard to find a grocery or a convenience store that didn't sell beer and wine. What were the church people to do? Not buy food?

Church law changed permitting members to shop at stores that sold beer and wine, but you could not shop in the aisle that shelves beer and wine. That worked for a time, until stores got smart setting up special displays of beer and wine in different areas of the store. There was great confusion as to where we were free to go, and where we were not to go. Soon, the rule was dropped. It became too complicated to clarify and enforce. The church relinquished allowing one to go down the aisle with beer and wine, but we were not to buy and consume it. Life settled into the new reality.

A few years later we faced a new war. A vote to legalize wine, beer, and spirits by the drink in restaurants, cafes, and bars confronted the church. Bars! We didn't have bars, but if the proposition passed, bars would be legal. The law passed. A new church law passed: "You do not go to restaurants that serve wine, beer, or spirits, and must we say anything about bars!" That didn't work for too long, as most of our favorite after-church-lunch restaurants began to sell wine and beer. Were we to abstain from eating out? Soon, social convention forced the final compromise: "You can dine in restaurants that serve alcohol; you, of course, shall not drink."

The church took a serious stand on the beverages. A radio announcer found himself excommunicated from our church for reading a beer commercial on radio! Imagine my fear a few years later when I was a disc jockey on a radio station that everybody in my church could hear. What if I got caught doing a beer commercial, or what if I just pushed the button that played a pre-recorded beer commercial? Would I be out?

Conversations around our dinner table with family and friends from the church always came around to the subject of drinking. I remember one lesson that I took to heart from listening in to these conversations: "It was better to be a flat-out drunk than to be a social drinker." I never figured out why.

Every year at Christmas, I watched a little mischief unfold in the Butler household. My dad, the chairman of the board of our church, and my mother a prominent soloist in the choir, indulged in a little drink. Sheepishly, my parents would recruit the services of a relative to purchase and secretly deliver a spirit to be added to the festive Christmas boiled custard—a thicker version of egg nog. I could tell my parents really enjoyed this little indulgence. You could also see a little guilt, but the smile of enjoyment prevailed. Many members of the church came by during the Christmas season to enjoy a little spiked boiled custard. It was good to see the good people at peace with joy—no war to fight. So what if my parents and their church friends enjoyed a little shot of bourbon in their custard.

I enjoyed watching the ritual every year for as far back as I can remember, and that goes back to the dry days in our county. I grew up around some good people, who were kind, helpful, and genuinely trying to be good Christians. It just always seemed faith was reduced to a list of things we were not to do.

Many of Jesus' parables and illustrations came from agriculture and often from wine, the vine, and the vineyard. The Old Testament is steeped in wine-knowledge, illustrations, and practical teaching such as how to plant a vineyard. Wine is one of the most cited subjects. Wine is an integral part of life throughout all ages of biblical history from Noah to Jesus to the disciples.

The spiritual journey's direction is a journey to freedom. If your journey is taking you in the opposite direction, that is not the way of the Spirit. The journey to freedom nourishes our desire to know more, to experience more, and to always ask the question: Is there something more to life—more beauty, more to know of God—our Source and provider? Is there more? Yes, there is always more!

"Do I have to stop drinking wine?" was the first question asked by a young man as he embarked on his spiritual journey as a follower of Jesus. I helped my friend search that question out for himself. Later he concluded that it was a non-issue, and that he was free to continue to enjoy wine as gift that is from God. It is a sad spiritual myth prevalent today that says, "To be spiritual a person must sacrifice all enjoyments and abandon anything that brings pleasure. Celebration is neglected, and life reduced to a mundane existence

On the other hand *wine creates moments*. Wine transforms ordinary events into occasions. On the occasion of my tenth wedding anniversary, my wife and I shared a bottle of wine together, in front of the fireplace on a typical cool, misty Oregon December night. For our novice palates, we enjoyed a sweeter German Riesling Ockfener-Bockstein, Mosel-Saar-Ruer Riesling Spatlese, 1976.

It was a spiritual experience—a creation experience— as the delicate floral aroma of a meadow with nuances of peach and apricot filled my nose as we enjoyed the crisp acicity and fruit. It was a theistic experience! It was a genuine expression of the goodness of God's creation and blessing, a flash of light creating a moment, and occasion. When I think back to that particular moment, I am reminded of the words of Galileo, "Wine is sunlight, held together by water."

I spent as many sunny afternoons in the vineyards and wineries surrounding my Oregon home as I could. The nearest winery to home, Oak Knoll up Burkhalter Road, was a favorite hangout to reflect and contemplate, and soak up some wine culture.

Through the years I've visited many of the great wine regions of the world from Burgundy, Champagne, Bordeaux, Tuscany, Spain, Napa, Sonoma, Washington State, New York, Australia, New Zealand, South Africa, Israel—and Oregon where my journey began. However far our journey takes us, there is always a warm place in our hearts for first places and first experiences.

Oak Knoll Winery is situated in the Tualatin Valley, near Portland, between the Coast Range Mountains to the west and the majestic Cascades to the east at the northern tip of the Willamette Valley. It is picturesque with a quilted mosaic of yellow and green fields intersected by forests and gentle rolling hills, and acres and acres of vineyards.

An electronics engineer started the winery to fulfill a personal dream. Oak Knoll was my introduction to Pinot Noir—the premier red grape of Oregon winemaking today. Like many wineries in the early days of Oregon's wine industry, there was a small tasting room and a few picnic tables on the grounds. It was a great place to learn about wine as the winemaker usually worked the tasting room, and was available to talk about wine and winemaking.

From those early days at Oak Knoll, the journey continued—discovering more about wine and life, wine and spirit, friendship, celebration, and God.

Now, I invite you to join me on a wine tour of the Bible and a spiritual experience—a "Wine and Spirit" tour. My purpose is simple: to introduce you to the Divine joy and permission to enjoy and celebrate wine as a gift and blessing from God. For you, who enjoy wine, but buy your wine looking over your shoulder, I hope you will begin to enjoy the God-given freedom, the invitation to pleasure in good things, and the times of celebration to the fullest. Those times don't just come. We have to be intentional. We create them.

I have no interest to persuade those who do not drink wine to begin. Enjoying wine is a gift, an invitation and a Divine permission, not a requirement. On the other hand to practice prohibition or abstinence is not a requirement, but is your freedom.

With glass in hand, read on. Discover. Find unexpected insights—surprisingly spiritual.

CHAPTER 2

IN THE BEGINNING

Wine cheers both God and Man. (Judges 9:13)

From Noah of the Bible to the people around our tables today, wine enriches lives. Wine helps turn an ordinary occasion into an extraordinary one. Wine turns an ordinary meal with friends into a celebration. Conversations with friends, glass in hand, become special. "Wine rejoices the heart of men, and joy is the mother of virtue," said German philosopher J.W. von Goethe.[1] Biblically speaking, wine accompanies friendship and stimulates conversation. Wine adds gusto to our appetites, "cheers" our spirits, energizes our passion for life, nurtures our souls, and replenishes our health.

Life in Bible times is intimately associated with the land and agriculture. The vineyard and wine were highly valued and a natural part of daily life, so much so, you'd have to say they lived in a wine culture. We need to keep this in mind as we read the Old and New Testament to understand fully the cultural context. People weren't sneaking around to drink wine, and they weren't looking over their shoulder hoping to not be discovered. They drank their wine in the presence of God. Wine was valued and drunk with proper decorum and moderation by the majority of people. Wine was central to their worship, their offerings to God, their feasts, and was known to be a sign of God's blessing.

The known existence of wine goes back as far as between 7000 and 5000 BCE. The first written account of viticulture and winemaking is in the Bible's Old Testament story of Noah.

Noah and his family landed on dry land after the great flood with their cargo of the many animals that God had told him to take. Noah was a husbandman—a man of the soil, a farmer. As such, he was experienced in the vineyard. It is likely that Noah carried grapevines aboard the ark. Even if he didn't carry vines, Noah surely obtained new vines that naturally returned from the ground after the flood. When the dove Noah sent out returned with an olive leaf, Noah knew that the land was dry.

After Noah was settled on dry land, he planted a vineyard. After the harvest and the fermentation of the grapes, wine was produced and Noah drank some. Noah drank too much wine on this occasion and became drunk. Noah's drunkenness was not the point of the story, and no condemnation of Noah was recorded. The biblical story of wine continues from there and the focus of the story of wine in the Bible remains grounded in enjoyment and blessing. While this is the emphasis, the Bible story of wine reminds us that there are consequences to abusing God's gift.

Some will use this story of Noah's drunkenness as a pretense for abstinence and prohibition from alcoholic beverages. But all that can be drawn from the story is that Noah grew vines, produced wine, drank wine, drank too much in this case, and became drunk. Noah is not condemned for growing the vines and producing wine.

The next scene in the Bible showed wine in a favorable and ceremonial light. Very little is known about the encounter of Melchizedek and Abram other than what is stated in the brief report found in Genesis 14:17-18. Abram had been blessed by God, and he returned from a military victory. Melchizedek, who was a priest of the Most High God came to Abram and blesses him in what must have been a time of jubilation, victory, and celebration. The ceremony included wine and bread that the priest brought out to Abram, and Abram drank the wine and ate the bread presented to him in commemoration and blessing.

The Old Testament references to wine continue in the same pattern. Wine was at the center of blessing and integral to celebration and joy.

In the Bible "wine" is used 234 times in 214 verses. Wine or the vine is mentioned in every book of the Old Testament except Jonah. Two-thirds of the verses concern blessings, enjoyment, celebrations, and religious ceremonies and offerings. One-third of the verses are remedial and warn of the consequences of abuse.

Celebrate!

God gave direction to the Israelites for a tithe in which they were to buy wine and strong drink for themselves and their families. The purpose of the tithe was to enjoy and celebrate in the presence of God! This command betrays the image of an overbearing God of no joy, of no enjoyment of life, of no goodness, and of no beauty.

The book of Deuteronomy records the remarkable command given to the Israelites. You can read the complete text for yourself in Deuteronomy 14:22-29.

> Be sure to set aside a tenth of all that your fields produce each year. Eat the tithe of your grain, new wine and oil, and the firstborn of your herds and flocks in the presence of the Lord your God... (Deuteronomy 14:22-23)

Sometimes this is called the "rejoicing tithe." God directed that the people set aside one-tenth of their wine and other possessions for their own to rejoice. In today's language you could call it a command to party in God's presence! Each family or household used the tithe to praise God in feasting and rejoicing. A purpose of this tithe was to impress on the people the importance of being joyful before the Lord being mindful of His goodness, faithfulness, love, and provision.

The location of the feast might make it impractical for those who lived too far away to bring a tenth of all their produce. The command said they could change their tithe from the agricultural goods to silver, so they could buy what they wanted for the feast. Here's the list of what they could buy with this tithe for themselves: cattle, sheep, wine, or other fermented drink, or anything else they wished.

The first Hebrew word for wine in Deuteronomy 14:26 is tiyrowsh, which is used more than fifty times in the Old Testament. Tiyrowsh refers to young wine that is not fully aged, but is fermented and intoxicating. (For a list of the different Hebrew and Greek words used for wine, see Appendix 1. Yayin is the most used Hebrew word for wine in the Old Testament, used 139 times.)

The second Hebrew word used here for "other fermented drink" is shekar. The verb form of the word means to be drunk or drunken. Shekar is used at times in a negative sense, as well as in a positive sense as in verse 26 and other passages, such as Proverbs 31:6. It is also translated as strong drink or fermented beverage, but it almost always means wine. Shekar here refers to other strong beverages, and was most likely referring to wine made from fruits other than grapes. Wine made from pomegranates during the time period of the Old Testament is mentioned in other historical sources. Shekar most likely refers to other kinds of wine, but some time the meaning is not certain. Shekar did not refer to distilled spirits. Distilled spirits were not known in these times.

From these Old Testaments events and instructions, it is clear that wine in the Bible is fermented beverage with intoxicating properties, and a gift of God to human beings for their enjoyment.

The Feast Of Booths

Now imagine one amazing celebration where the rejoicing tithe of Deuteronomy 14 was applied. The Feast of Booths (temporary dwellings) or Feast of Tabernacles as it was also called—was probably the most popular and joyful feast celebrated by the Hebrew people. The feast was a reminder that the Jewish people had lived in booths when they were brought out of slavery in Egypt. The feast lasted one whole week! By our modern calendar, the feast occurred annually around the end of October when grape and fruit crops were harvested.

Do you think it is a legitimate lifestyle we live today in North American culture—that we work hard and long, with an annual short vacation of a week or two for most people? Does our perceived complexity of life legitimately require a sustained work mode? Where would a week-long celebration, a party if you please, fit into most of our schedules? Maybe, at Christmas! It would benefit us to set a regular time to relax, contemplate, celebrate, and reflect on our lives. Do you need to make some changes to insure that celebration and enjoyment are part of your life?

The scene at the Feast of Tabernacles would look something like this: The people gathered in a place designated by God. They camped in gardens, fields, rooftops, tents and booths made from branches, as a reminder that they lived in booths when they had been brought out of slavery in Egypt. It was a happy and festive occasion. The work of harvest had ended. Normal work was suspended to focus on celebrating before God. I am sure children were caught up in this atmosphere, and ran and played freely. Families and friends ate generous meals together, and relaxed with wine or other "strong drinks" in the presence of God. The feast wasn't just for the affluent. The wealthy families were to share with the poorer at the feast so they could fully participate in the celebration.

The feast was a holy convocation where offerings and special sacrifices were made. As a symbol, water was poured out and prayers for good rains for the next season were offered to God. There was anticipation for the next year's harvests expecting, once again, God's blessing of an abundant harvest. The Feast of Booths was one festive campout. This celebration has no equivalent in modern Christianity.

Wine contributed to the spirit of the celebration, and was drunk in praise and thanksgiving for God's provision. The feast demonstrated that wine was good and could be enjoyed in the presence of God. There was no guilt or condemnation for drinking wine. It was joyous occasion with God at the center!

The Nazirite And Abstinence

In the Bible, abstinence from wine was required in a specific situation and that for a limited time. We are not given much information about the Nazirite and the Naziritic vow. All of sudden instructions for the Nazirite appear in the book of Numbers in Chapter 6. We know from the text that a Nazirite was a class of people especially devoted to God. The name Nazirite in Hebrew means consecration, devotion, and separation. One of the most popularly known Nazirites is Samson.

The Nazirite made a vow for a specific period of time for special service and devotion to God. It is suggested that 30 days was the typical period, but there are indications that the time period varied. During the period of the vow, the Nazirite was not to drink wine or any strong alcoholic drink. The Nazirite was also to abstain from raisins, vinegar, and nuts.

This Naziritic vow was the only spiritual context where abstinence from wine was a requirement. When the time of the vow ended, it was marked by a prescribed ritual, and the Nazirite could drink wine once again. The Naziritic vow was an aberration of normal life, a special exception. The case of the Nazirite is not a pretense for requiring abstinence from drinking wine, and is not a basis for prohibition.

There is one other case where a group of people abstained from wine, and that was for life. The people were the Rechabites called to a nomadic way of life. To plant vineyards and make wine would require a settled way of life contrary to their calling as a people, since this form of nomadic life stemmed from a vow of asceticism. Abstinence, then, did reflect a unique feature of Rechabite life.

Application of the Nazirite principle of abstaining from wine for the purpose of a special focus and devotion to God for a period of time can be a positive, beneficial, and meaningful spiritual practice. For the pace at which we live with multitasking, information overload, and trying to be everywhere at once—omnipresence—it is a good practice to pull away to regain our awareness, our spirit, and our consciousness of God.

Abstaining not only from wine, but also refraining from activity and spending a period of time in silence can provide spiritual renewal, nurture, and refreshment. The Psalmist encourages us to "Be still and know that I am God."

At other times, wine can be a part of our spiritual practice when we come together with others in community for communion, contemplation, reflection, and raising our awareness of God. Wine does symbolize God's blessing and provision. Each time you drink wine, you participate in the goodness of God's creation. It is an act of receiving the blessing and provision from God—a blessing delivered in many varieties!

CHAPTER 3

WINES OF ALL KINDS

In that day the mountains will drip new wine...
(Joel 3:18)

The Wines Of The Old Testament

What wine might our Old Testament spiritual predecessors have enjoyed? There wasn't Merlot, Chardonnay, Cabernet Sauvignon, or other varieties of wine we know today, but the Bible reveals an advanced level of knowledge about varieties and styles of wine, and winemaking. Wine known in Bible times is more than generic red jug wines. Wines of place, style, and age were known and enjoyed. A survey of wine descriptions in the Old Testament tells of diversity and appreciation of wines of all kinds.

Other historical sources collaborate the presence of a wide variety of styles of wine in the time period of the Bible—from Noah all the way to Jesus' day.

Athenaeus in his classical work *The Sages at Dinner* written between 200 and 228 BCE gave an extensive list of different wines.[2] A commentator on Greek life and historian, he provides a colorful insight into Greek culture and customs. Athenaeus relied on older written works for his catalog of wines. It seems his list of wines includes wines that had been around from the early days of Greek dominance of the wine trade, maybe listing wines from the sixth to fifth centuries BCE that were still around at the writing of the Sages.

Biblical wine history predates that of the Greeks and Romans, and tells of local wines from what is now modern

Israel, as well as referring to wines from other places as we shall see. The Old Testament time period ends at 400 BCE when the Greeks were the dominant wine producers. Four centuries later when Jesus came, the Romans were supplanting Greece as the dominant wine producer.

Citing other ancient sources *The Wine Route of Israel* speaks of the diversity of wines referring to times a few centuries after Jesus to the time of the Talmud (around 500 CE):

> *A surprising wide range of wines existed in ancient times. The Talmud refers to sixty types of wine, discussing them in terms of their quality, value and use. In classical literature, many more varieties are mentioned. Pliny, the Roman writer list 80 types of wine, and the geographer Strabo lists as many as 130.*[3]

The extensive selection of wines suggests people had a choice of wines for any occasion, purpose, or specific meal!

The following Old Testament categories reflect the nature, diversity, place, and style of wines from the ancient days of Noah to around four hundred years before Jesus.

Wine Or Other Fermented Drink

In Deuteronomy 14:26, Deuteronomy 29:6, and Judges 13:4,7 wine is described as a fermented beverage. It's not unfermented grape juice. Grape juice might have been consumed immediately at harvest, but after that, there was no way to preserve juice other than fermentation into wine—after all, Louis Pasteur's discovery was centuries away! Grape juice is a late invention. Evidence for wine being anything less than fermented beverage doesn't exist.

Wines Of All Kinds

At the time of the great leader Nehemiah, many years after Noah and Abram, a variety of wines were available. In the Bible, Nehemiah, Chapter 5, gives an account of food and wine supplies for more than 150 people that dined at Nehemiah's table each day. The account tells that "every ten days an abundant supply of wines of all kinds" was brought in for Nehemiah's table. The wines of all kinds included wines blended with spices, and included wine made from fruit other than grapes. Wines of all kinds would include young wines and older wines. While evidence would suggest wines of this time were red, there's ample information that strongly suggest the presence of white wines as well.

Nehemiah served in the government of Persia under King Artaxerxes I. Nehemiah's post was that of cup-bearer to the king. His responsibility was to taste the king's wine to make sure it wasn't poisoned! No doubt, Nehemiah tasted plenty of wine, but not in the ideal context for a wine tasting! Nehemiah was more than a cup-bearer, even though that was one of his tasks. He was essentially second in command of Persia—a Secretary of State as such. The citation of the supplies provided Nehemiah, and his role as cup-bearer show that wine was ubiquitous in life and society.

Once, visiting friends in the southwestern corner of Germany, I was served a local wine believed to have originated in the Jordan Valley thousands of years ago. The white wine we were drinking was Gudetel.[4] Gudetel is grown in this region and in Switzerland where it is known as Chasselas. Gudetel produces a refreshing, crisp white wine. My friends were part of a church, Freie Evangelische Geemeinde Rebland. The church ran a restaurant that served wine from a winery owned and operated by one of the church members. Gudetel was one of the wines of the winery. Sipping Gudetel with these friends, I was conscious of the connection of the wine to biblical times and place. I was also excited to discover a Protestant church with a wine connection! The name of the church, Gemeinde Rebland translated to English means the *Winelands Church*—an appropriate name! It remains a memorable moment along my journey.

Unfortunately, as is true with many regional wines, Gudetel is not available in the US, nor is it produced in its native home Palestine. If you travel, one of the joys of wine is discovering local wines that are rarely distributed outside the local area. So, if you get to Southwest Germany, try a bottle of Gudetel. It may be one of the "wines of all kinds" in the Bible.

Blended, Mixed, And Spiced Wine

Song of Songs is a series of lyric poems that can make one blush with lines like, "Your navel is a rounded goblet that never lacks blended wine," Song 7:2. (emphasis added) It is a beautiful description of lovers and their passion for one another. The Song is an appropriate setting to connect wine with love and the celebration that accompanies the love between two people.

The poems celebrate the beauty and wonder of human love, and there is an honest and open delight in physical attraction. The Song draws the connection between wine and the beauty of love? God sees it. It is written in the Bible complete with frequent references to wine—"…and your mouth like the best wine. Beloved, may the wine go straight to my lover, flowing gently over lips and teeth." The Song tells us that love is better than wine, "For your love is more delightful than wine." Few things are better than wine, but we must concede to love!

At the beginning of the Song, blended wine is mentioned in poetic description. Blended and mixed wine were mixed with a variety of herbs and spices, and may not be referencing blends of various grapes—although that can't be completely ruled out. (The more I study wine in ancient history, the clearer the evidence that good, elegant wines existed, and the practice of blending different grapes to make wine was known.)

Blending wine with spices was a common practice and shows early development of the art of winemaking. Some of these herbs and spices produced highly intoxicating wines. Wine was mixed with myrrh making a stupefying blended wine—like an anesthesia. Myrrh was valued for perfume, which is why it was presented as a gift to the baby Jesus. Wine mixed with myrrh was offered to Jesus on the cross, but he refused to take it. Wine mixed with myrrh, because of its anesthetic effect, would have helped relieve Jesus' suffering. (See Chapter 8)

Isaiah 65:11 describes a feast God would spread for his people. God was calling his people who had ignored and forgotten him. Part of their intended destiny was to feast with God. It was a feast featuring bowls of mixed wine. The condition for such a feast was a heart for God, and faithfulness to the way of life they were called to live. God wanted the people to feast, drink wine, and enjoy him.

Bottled-Up Wine

In Job 32:19 Elihu told Job that he "is like bottled-up wine." He said he is full of words for Job and is about to explode to get those words out. "Inside I am like bottled-up wine, like new wineskins ready to burst."

Elihu was familiar with the properties of wine. Fermentation continues, or more likely secondary fermentation, after the wine is in the wineskin. Carbon dioxide, a byproduct of the fermentation process, exerts pressure on the skin as if it were bottled-up. Wine went through the first fermentation in jars due to the violent nature of the process—the pressure would likely burst the strongest wineskins.

The Gospel of Mark (2:22) in the New Testament uses the same imagery to describe the problem of pouring new wine into old wineskins. Again, new wine is too active in the fermentation process, and the old skins lack elasticity to withstand the pressure that is exerted on the wineskin during fermentation. While not so much a kind or style of wine, the description gives insight into wine knowledge and practice in the day of Job.

Aged Wine

"On this mountain the LORD Almighty will prepare a feast of rich food for all peoples, a banquet of aged wine—the best of meats and the finest of wines" reads Isaiah 25:6.

So, what about aged wine? An aged wine has achieved balance between all of its parts—acidity, sweetness, the fruit and tannin, and that makes the wine silky smooth. All the components of the wine are in harmony. It is mostly red wine that has the potential for aging, but some white wine of the day might have some aging potential.

Have you ever taken a sip of red wine that makes you pucker and dries up your mouth? That's the sensation of tannin in the wine. Tannin is a substance that comes naturally from the woody part of the grape—the skins and pips (seeds)—and from the oak barrels used for aging wines in modern winemaking. In making red wine, the skins and pips are left in contact with the juice, introducing the tannin into the wine. Tannin is not a taste. It is a tactile sensation. In young and more complex red wines, tannin makes you pucker, because the tannins are in a round shape that allows them to penetrate into your taste buds, easily producing the pucker effect. As the wine ages, the tannins elongate and cannot penetrate into the taste buds as they could when young and rounded. Now the wine slides across the taste buds with silky smoothness in balance.

The desire for aged-wine and the special place of aged-wine in the Bible is referenced more than once. The fact that aged-wine was served at the special feasts, banquets, and other special gatherings show the value and appreciation of aged-wine. How old were the aged-wines? We can't say with any certainty. Answers vary from one or two years to three or more. Aged-wines were not as finessed and smooth as wines today, but were certainly superior to the young wines, which were consumed soon after the harvest. Yet, the new wine was a cause for celebration too. The harvest and the advent of new wine brought its own celebration!

Today, a one-year-old-wine would not be considered old or aged, but considering ancient Palestine's climate and hygienic conditions, a one-year-old-wine might be considered old. Today, only around five-percent of wine produced is for aging. Ninety-five percent of wine is made for immediate off-the-shelf consumption. One market study says that a bottle of wine is consumed within ten hours of leaving the shelf in the US.

Wine Left On Its Dregs (Lees)

Jeremiah 48:11 describes wine left on its lees, as does Zephaniah 1:12. This is wine that is "complacent...like wine left on its dregs (lees)." Lees or dregs are heavier particles, sediment that forms during the fermentation process and settles to the bottom of the container. Wine left to rest on its lees is a technique employed by winemakers to develop a richer, fuller-tasting wine.

Winemakers today use this technique to add complexity and to develop a richer flavor—often with California Chardonnays. In the Jeremiah text, the wine left on its lees was contrasted to wine poured from one jar to another. What does that mean? Wine was poured from the initial jar where the wine was first fermented, and then it was poured into another jar for a secondary fermentation. The wine remains "complacent" resting on its sediment for an extended period of time. Wine left on its lees is considered a superior wine.

Wine From Lebanon

In Hosea 14:7, the prophet Hosea's mention of the wine of Lebanon identifies the wine as famed.

> *Men will dwell again in his shade. He will flourish like the grain. He will blossom like a vine, and his fame will be like the wine of Lebanon.*

The prophet was calling Israel back to God, and described the blessings to come from their turning. In honoring God, the people of Israel would blossom like a vine, and their fame would be like the wine of Lebanon! At the time of the prophet (around the mid 8th century BCE) the wine of Lebanon was known to be some of the best! Hosea could use the analogy knowing it would be understood. Israel's blessing upon returning to

God would esteem them as a great people like the famed wine of Lebanon.

In Lebanon today, of the more than 66,000 acres planted to grapes, about 37,000 are planted to wine grapes—the remainder for table grapes.[5] The slopes of the Bekaa Valley are the center of wine cultivation in Lebanon. Mostly red grapes are planted and varieties include Cinsault, Carignan, Mourverde, Grenache, Alicante, and the more familiar Cabernet Sauvignon and Syrah. Whites include Chardonnay, Sauvignon Blanc, and Semillon.

The twenty years of civil war in Lebanon nearly destroyed the wine industry. Demand for wine plummeted locally, and due to the hostilities, most wineries were unable to harvest their crops. One remarkable winery was able to continue operation. Chateau Musar[6] continued to produce wines throughout the years of conflict and continues today. Chateau Musar wines are available in the US, and you can locate wine merchants on the internet that sell Lebanese wines. When you want to feel a little closer to your spiritual roots, try a Chateau Musar wine or any wine from Lebanon, and experience the fame of the wine of Lebanon, just as they were in biblical times.

Find a Lebanese or Middle-Eastern restaurant that serves wines from Lebanon for a different wine experience.

Wine From Helbon

Wine from where? Helbon, would be just outside the modern-day city of Damascus, Syria. Helbon is mentioned one time in a lament for Tyre—an important center at the time of the prophet Ezekiel, who began his prophetic ministry around 593 BCE. The prophet was leading up to condemnation of the conduct of Tyre. As he did so, he talked of all the centers of the day that were trading with Tyre, including Helbon: "Damascus, because of your many products and great wealth of goods, did business with you in wine from Helbon, and wool from Zahar" (Ezekiel 27:18).

Helbon is believed to be the modern village Helbun in modern-day Syria. About 13 miles northwest of Damascus, Helbon supplied wine to Damascus for trading with Tyre. Tyre possessed many valued goods that were needed in Damascus, so Damascus, by necessity, traded with Tyre. The wine of Helbon met the criteria of a product worthy of trade with Tyre. Other historical sources tell that the wine of Helbon was supplied to King Nebuchadnezzar for sacrificial purposes, and was known to be a favorite wine of the kings of Persia. Wine of Helbon might have been included in the supplies for Nehemiah mentioned in Nehemiah 5.

The Old Testament tells a story of wines of many styles, quality, and age, as well as wines distinguished by place, such as Lebanon and Helbon, and Palestine itself. Wines of all kinds were available throughout the lands of biblical history.

CHAPTER 4

OF GOODNESS AND BLESSING

May God give you of heaven's dew and of earth's richness—an abundance of grain and new wine. (Genesis 27:28)

The Celebration

The winepress and the threshing floor were symbols that vividly reminded God's people of his goodness and blessing. Through the abundance of grain, olives, and new wine, the dance of creation—where Creator and human labor came together each year—brought about an exclamation point of blessing!

> *They will come and shout for joy on the heights of Zion: they will rejoice in the bounty of the Lord—the grain, the new wine and the oil, the young of the flocks and herds. They will be like a well-watered garden... (Jeremiah 31:12)*

In contrast, the Bible describes the empty threshing floor and the empty winepress in bleak terms of brokenness between the Creator and his people.

> *Joy and gladness are gone from the orchards and fields of Moab. I have stopped the flow of wine from the presses: no one treads them with shouts of joy. Although there are shouts, they are not shouts of joy. (Jeremiah 48:33)*

Sadness that the flow of wine has stopped shows how wine was such a part of daily life and how highly it was valued. It was understood that the new wine evidenced God's blessing. One can imagine the joyful spirit, the singing and shouting at the winepress each year for a successful harvest.

To be present at a winery at harvest time is an exciting experience. Soaking in the atmosphere and activities that go along with the harvest and the crush is as joyful a time today, as it was a joyful time of celebration in biblical times. The only thing missing is the crushing of the grapes by foot. Even with modern technology we possess today, there are places that continue to press the grapes by foot including Portugal's famed port-producing region along the Duaro River. Guests are invited to participate in the age-old practice of crushing the grapes by foot.

The modern winery features state of the art technology that saves time and labor. Mechanized crushers replace crushing the grapes by foot, but modern technology doesn't diminish the fun at harvest time. Autumn is a great time to visit wineries, when some of the new vintage bottlings are released. It's one way to relive the experience people from biblical times had as they celebrated the new wine. In addition, many wineries stage concerts, dances, and all kinds of celebrations soon after the harvest. Many feature tasting of their new wines to welcome the new vintage.

The Old Testament harvests were happy times. Harvest provided a powerful visual reminding everyone of their source of provision. New wine expresses another season of God's goodness and blessing. A trip to the supermarket or the wine store doesn't make for a very powerful reminder that God is our source of provision and abundance. Our lives are so separated from the miracle of God's provision that the closest we come to the source of our food is the trip to the supermarket.

I think those who labored in the vineyards and made wine in ancient times would trade their challenging labor for modern equipment to assist them in the process of picking, crushing, and bottling among other tasks. I'm equally sure that they would not want to trade the festivities and celebrations of the harvest for a trip to the store. A trip to the store is not exactly a meaningful moment. So much of our modern lifestyle separates us from the enjoyment of moments such as the harvesting of grapes for the new vintage.

The romance of picking grapes by hand and crushing the grapes by foot is for the imagination of the separated, modern-suburban mind. Separated in the reality that the closest most of us get to our food sources is the supermarket, where the work of winemaking is already bottled, and our meat, well, nicely packaged in clear plastic.

The Winepress

Isaiah 5:1-2 describes the preparation and planting of a vineyard. One of the tasks was to "cut out a winepress" as translated in the *New International Version (NIV) Bible*. The word "cut" means "to dig." At first, the action of digging a winepress puzzled me.

Matthew 21:33 and Mark 12:1 include the same description of digging a winepress. Digging a wine press at the time of Isaiah's writing, and in the parable that Jesus taught are the same.

The winepress was hewn out of rock, but in some places, in the absence of rock, it was dug in the ground. If you have traveled to Israel and the Middle East, you can see why a winepress hewn in rock was logical, sensible, and ingenious. Much of the land is rocky terrain.

Many of these ancient presses are evident today. While the size of the presses varied, there were some consistencies: a rectangular or circular floor was cut into the rock two to three feet deep. There were two floors, one higher than the other and connected to the lower floor by a channel of some kind for the juice to flow down. The wider and shallower upper level was the main press. This is where the grapes were crushed by foot. The juice flowed down to the lower floor where it was put into jars, or in some cases the juice was left on the second floor for the first fermentation. Because of the heat in Palestine, the fermentation would begin immediately on the floor of the press.

It was not unusual for a winepress to have a third level, allowing for some settling and straining of the juice. Wooden beams were sometimes used to finish the pressing. The winepress, carved out of stone, worked serving the process from grapes to juice to fermentation to wine! A great deal of know-how and commitment to sound practices to produce good wine was strongly suggested by the details given in the Bible from "digging a winepress" to the fermentation process. A winepress cut into rock would work today. I live on rocky land, and I've been thinking, "I should try to dig a winepress!"

Harvest time was a time of long hours of labor, but also was a time to recognize God's provision—a time of festive celebration and anticipation of the new wine soon to come. Those are spiritual moments! As we saw earlier, harvest time preceded the most popular of the Jewish feasts—The Feast of Booths or Tabernacles:

> *Celebrate the Feast of Tabernacles for seven days after you have gathered the produce of your threshing floor and your winepress. (Deuteronomy 16:13)*

The feast lasted seven days! Few today take a seven-day vacation!

The cycle of agriculture gave life a rhythm—seasons of planting, growing, harvesting, and resting—the latter is the missing season of modern life. Rest!

Molded by structures of industrialization, bureaucratization, and the accompanying technology to measure time in millionths of a second, we have been forced into a chronic season of work. Many rarely experience any sense of harvest, and rest is a lost art. Are we not robbed of a life-rhythm that is us—humans created in the Image of God?

We are now sadly devoid of seasons, that human rhythm that provides a season of rest, reflection, and celebration. Without rest, when do we drink our wine?

Dividing our life into such shortened measures of time—days, hours, minutes, and seconds is disorienting, and debilitating causing us to set unreasonable goals and expectations. The consequent condition is impatience. Constantly measuring time is not a spiritual rhythm. The micro-measurement of time produces a staccato of un-rhythmic, syncopated movements that make us spill our wine! Must we hurry from the winepress to tomorrow's tasks…everyday?

Heaven's Dew

Genesis 27:28 is a prayer that describes wine as "heaven's dew." The prayer was for God's provision to Jacob for an abundance of grain and new wine—heaven's dew—a fitting biblical description for wine.

As heaven's dew, wine was worthy and acceptable as an offering to God. Leviticus 23:13 prescribed a "quarter of a hin of wine" as part of an acceptable offering made to God. (A hin is the equivalent of about one U.S. gallon.) Other offerings called for a half of a hin. Throughout the Old Testament wine was prescribed over and over as an acceptable offering to God.

I mentioned earlier that in the hot Palestine days, grape juice would immediately begin to ferment right on the press floor. According to Jewish tradition when the first foam appeared on the surface of the liquid, which occurred on the first day, the wine was then accountable to the wine tithe. The stipulation confirms how rapidly initial fermentation took place. There was little time for grape juice! Heaven's dew was forming—actually foaming. You can drink your heaven's dew as a personal drink-offering to the Most High God, as an expression from the heart honoring God our provider.

How The Bible Categorizes Wine

He makes grass grow for the cattle, and plants for us to cultivate—bringing forth food from the earth: wine that

gladdens the heart of man, oil to make his face shine,
and bread that sustains his heart. (Psalm 104:14-15)

Wine is food! Psalm 104 speaks of God's provision and care for us. We see the providential care, which God exercises over creation. We experience God's faithfulness in wine! Hebrew scholars say that the Psalm refers to two main staples of life: wine and bread! From the Hebrew, the text should read, "And wine that gladdens the heart of man so as to make his face shine more than oil, and bread that sustains the heart." No doubt that olive oil was one of the three staples of life, but here, this Psalmist emphasizes wine and bread. The significance of wine and bread is familiar to followers of Jesus, as in our various traditions we celebrate the Lord's Supper or Holy Communion in remembrance of what Jesus has done for us with bread and wine.

Wine is a life-giving food of such benefit that it makes our face shine more than oil. When we pray and thank God for provision, we can give thanks for our food—our wine, our bread, and all other food he faithfully provides.

Proverbs And Wine

Think of Proverbs as a series of maxims—wise sayings or general truths about life. In *Eerdman's Handbook to the Bible*, Derek Kidner gives a succinct description of Proverbs:

> *Proverbs is a book of wise sayings: not simply an anthology, but an oriental textbook, schooling…in wise and right living by the repetition of wise thoughts. It is wisdom distilled into short, sharp phrases, dramatic contrasts, and unforgettable scenes from life.*[7]

Proverbs belongs to the era of the kings of Israel, dating back, perhaps, to between 1000-900 BCE. Authorship of Proverbs is attributed to King Solomon. The instruction and wisdom regarding wine drinking was developed over a long period time period of observation and experience.

Here's a contemporary tale of modern proverbs. Working with a group of missionaries in Europe, I came across a letter from the leader of a US mission agency to his people in the field. The letter instructed them to be good missionaries by "abstaining from sexual immorality, not drinking wine, and being good Americans."[8] The first is good. The second, humorous—given that these missionaries served in one of the wine regions of the world where drinking wine was part of Christian life, and not an issue. The letter got into the hands of local Christian leaders, who graciously rolled their eyes and could only say, "You Americans." And it was said with grace and respect.

On another occasion, a breakthrough moment helped to further free my spirit. One evening in the small French village of Gex, just across the border with Geneva, Switzerland, I attended what to me was an old-fashioned church "potluck" dinner. We had them all the time in the churches in the South, but there was a different twist to this night's gathering.

The dinner was with a church group in the village getting together for a meal. People were coming to the church each family bringing a dish of food—and a bottle of wine—to share with each other at the meal! Even though I was a wine drinker, this differed from any other experience I'd had at a church-sponsored meal.

I asked one of my friends at the church about this. "Oh, yes, we often have a dinner like this and everyone brings a dish and a favorite wine." It was another memorable experience— an evening of community, food, and wine with my French and Swiss Christian friends.

Ten years earlier, I would have been a little distracted by the drinking of wine at a church event. I would have missed the genuine love and community these people experienced together. I drank wine, but this was my first wine drinking at a church event. I would have been just like the Pharisee who missed the point, when he couldn't see Jesus for whom he was; he could only see Jesus' dirty hands because he did not wash them ceremonially according to religious law.

A modern Proverb our society needs to heed today is, "Lighten up!"

Many Christians in North America argue for abstention or prohibition from drinking wine or any alcoholic drink. So be it. I have chosen to write about the joys of wine as God's gift that is constantly affirmed in the Bible. On so many issues, maybe it is time we lightened up to enjoy some of what God provides for our enjoyment and celebration of life—that Jesus said was to a life of abundance!

The argument put forward by most prohibitionists and proponents of abstinence is that if it can be abused, don't use. The argument is really silly and selectively used. Have you heard that we should prohibit and abstain from food? Food can be and is abused. From money? Money can be and is abused. Knowledge? It can be used and is abused. Kenneth L. Gentry in *God Gave Wine* points out the parallel with 1 Corinthians 8:1, which says, "knowledge makes arrogant." Gentry comments further on the argument:

> Obviously neither Christian ethics nor a biblical world view disparages the quest for knowledge....In certain respects wine-consumption and knowledge-acquisition are similar, and bring certain responsibilities with them. That is, each can be used for either good or evil. The point of Proverbs is that wine has the potential to mock, just as the point of Paul is that knowledge has the potential to make arrogant.[9]

Think of all the good things God provides. Can you think of any of those good things that cannot be abused? The argument would eliminate life all together!

The wisdom of Proverbs provides wise insights into the enjoyment of wine, and doesn't neglect to warn about abusing wine.

Proverbs Warning About Abusing Wine

The following proverbs speak to abusing wine in witty word pictures.

"Wine is a mocker and beer a brawler; whoever is led astray by them is not wise," Proverbs 20:1. That we should not be enslaved to wine is the point of the proverb. It is not a prohibition to drinking wine and beer, but again, a warning to be vigilant to not overindulge. Again, Gentry says:

> Wine is a joyful reward to those obedient to God. (Deut. 14:26) Wine, which in the drunkard's life is a "brawler," is in the poetry of God an emblem of blessing. (Amos 9:13-15)

"He who loves pleasure will become poor; whoever loves wine and oil will never be rich," Proverbs 21:17. Here, loving pleasure, wine, and oil refer to obsession and overindulgence—a life inordinately consumed by these. The meaning of the text is not abstinence or prohibition. Biblical scholars mostly agree, but many will then go on to argue that the Bible is telling us what will happen if we simply drink wine. Drinking wine or beer, they say, is a slide down the slippery slope to a life of debauchery, drunkenness, and wasted living.

> Do not join those who drink too much wine or gorge themselves on meat, those who linger over wine, who go to sample bowls of mixed wine. (Proverbs 23:20)

This makes the point I'm emphasizing: don't overindulge. I think we get the picture, but let's look at one more proverb—Proverbs 23:30-31, the favorite text of prohibitionist and advocates of abstention:

> Do not gaze at wine when it is red,
> when it sparkles in the cup,
> when it goes down smoothly!

In the end it bites like a snake,
and poisons like a viper.

It's a vivid word picture about one who is over indulging in wine. Consistent with Proverbs and throughout the Bible, the warning is to not abuse wine. It is not a call to prohibit or abstain.

One final note—Solomon states that he pursued wine and folly as ultimate sources for happiness (Ecclesiastes 2:3). Solomon was searching for meaning to life: "I wanted to see what was worthwhile for us to do under heaven during the few days of our lives." In his deliberations, Solomon rejects the idea that happiness can come from a life consumed with wine and folly. Solomon realized a life spent obsessed and captive to wine and folly is obviously foolish.

Yet driven as we are today, we are precariously hydroplaning through life never still enough to be present with ourselves, our friends, our God, and Creation—that can be gladly accompanied by a good glass of wine. We miss what makes life worthwhile with busyness, even busyness in the name of God. Discover that there is a "time for everything, a season for every activity."

Solomon in his search for meaning did not condemn wine, but condemned the folly of building our lives around wine as well as "embracing folly" period. Solomon instructs, "...drink your wine with a joyful heart," and says, "...wine makes life merry." It's common sense. Abusing drink is reckless. The moderate consumption of wine is part of an abundant life.

Throughout the Old Testament, wine is described as a blessing and a gift from God. Wine and celebration are good things, even encouraged. Wine is food for our table. Wine reminds us of goodness, beauty, and truth. When we see goodness, beauty, and truth, we see God. After the last word of the Old Testament comes Jesus, and who doesn't know Jesus' first miracle—performed at a wedding in Cana!

CHAPTER 5

WHAT WOULD JESUS DRINK?

Wine In The New Testament

They offered Jesus wine to drink… (Matthew 27:34)

So much of life takes place around food and drink—they are the consummate accompaniment to being with one another. This is true when Jesus lived on earth as it is today. The four New Testament Gospels depict a Jesus who socializes with all kinds of people, and frequently in settings that include food and drink.

In the times of Jesus, wine was a regular part of most everyone's diet. Wine was spoken of in the normal course of the stories and narratives of the New Testament. Throughout the New Testament, scenes of everyday life were played out describing encounters with Jesus. Jesus came into the mainstream of everyday human existence. He did not live an esoteric and detached life, but one fully engaged with people—connected, caring, and compassionate—yet Jesus was transcendently different. He astounded, and surely confused his early followers, when he said, "When you see me, you are seeing God!"

The Demon And The Drunkard

One day Jesus was talking with people, and some religious leaders called Pharisees were within hearing distance. In the conversation, Jesus described how these religious leaders said that John the Baptist was demonic, and how they called him (Jesus) a glutton and a drunkard. "John the Baptist came neither eating bread nor drinking wine, and you say, 'He has a demon.' The Son of Man (Jesus) came eating and drinking, and you say, 'Here is a glutton and a drunkard, a friend of tax collectors and sinners.'" (Luke 7:33-34 paraphrased)

Jesus came eating and drinking—so much so, that the Pharisees felt they had reason to call Jesus a drunkard! The Pharisees were a self-appointed religious sect made up of Rabbinic teachers of the law, who were not priests. As a matter of fact, they formed because they felt the formal priesthood had fallen into a bankrupt and corrupt state, and they, the Pharisees, had it right, and would straighten everyone else out.

Pharisee literally means, "separated ones," and they lived separated from the mainstream of society, since they saw themselves as superior to everyone else.

They had codified the Torah[10] (Old Testament Law) into specific and defined behavior, so that the rules were impossible for others to keep. And if you could not keep their rules, you were wrong, unholy, and unspiritual in their eyes. The results of their fanatical demands for what they construed to be right crushed the spirit of most people—literally the letter of their law crushed the spirit of the law. The Pharisees constantly harangued everyone and especially Jesus, because he did not practice their exacting rites and rituals. The Pharisees were hyper-critical, judgmental, and condemning of those who did not keep the law as they did. The Pharisees constantly debated and challenged Jesus on everything he said and did. They condemned Jesus as a glutton and a drunkard, and condemned another prophet—John The Baptist as demon possessed!

John The Baptist was not identified as a Nazarite, although his lifestyle did parallel the requirements of a Nazarite. The angel who announced the coming birth of John told the father-to-be that John would be a joy and delight, and "great in the sight of the Lord." The angel went on to say, "He is never to take wine or other fermented drink...." Abstaining from wine was a requirement of the Nazaritic vow for the time period of the vow. A Nazarite was committed to a special mission or consecration before God for a period of time until the purpose of the vow was completed.

The fact that John was never to take wine is unusual for a Nazarite. Perhaps this unique requirement was because the mission of John The Baptist was like no other, so the vow was for a lifetime.

John the Baptist's special mission was to tell the people of Jesus' coming, and that Jesus was the long-anticipated Messiah. Because of his vow, John the Baptist abstained from wine, bread, and the other required abstentions like that of a Nazarite such as nuts and raisins. Reflecting the simple life of a Nazarite, John ate a diet of locusts and honey, and wore clothing made of camels' hair with a leather girdle. Because of this, the religious leaders said he was weird—perhaps even demon-possessed.

Because, according to the charge of the Pharisees against Jesus—that Jesus drank wine and ate bread, these same "religious" men called him a drunkard and a glutton, and they condemned him for hanging out with the "wrong" crowd. Between the Pharisees' criticism of John and Jesus on both ends of the behavioral spectrum, no middle ground is left for anyone to measure up and be accepted—except the Pharisees themselves in their self-declared "righteousness!"

It is tempting to say that the Pharisees characterization of Jesus and John and by the arguments of contemporary abstentionist and neo-prohibitionists, those who enjoy wine today are drunkards and gluttons, and the abstentionist and prohibitionist are demon possessed!

From the charges of the Pharisees and New Testament descriptions of Jesus' encounters with people, three conclusions about the life of Jesus are evident:

Jesus ate the normal diet of the day.

Jesus ate and drank with all kinds of people, including the non-religious.

Jesus drank wine.

Followers after Jesus strive to reflect the character of Jesus in their lives, desire to act and live as he did, and strive to align their mind and behavior with his. In every situation, the follower of Jesus asks "What would Jesus do?" And now we ask, "What would Jesus drink?"

Jesus Goes To A Party

Then Levi had a great banquet for Jesus at his house, and a large crowd of tax collectors and others were eating with them. (Luke 5:29)

Jesus went to see Levi (Matthew) at his tax office, and challenged him to "follow" him (Jesus). It seems that Levi had some immediate enlightenment in the encounter with Jesus. Right away Matthew organized a banquet—a party with Jesus as guest of honor. At the party was a large crowd of his fellow tax collectors and others. I speculate that the others were a very interesting group. Matthew doesn't hang out with religious people!

Gatherings of this nature in homes were not unusual in Jewish culture, but the mix at Matthew's party was unusual. First, there's Matthew's friends—fellow tax collectors. Back then, tax collectors were the most hated class of people. They were Jews, but collected taxes for the occupying Romans. They earned their income by what they could extort from their countrymen, and Matthew wanted these friends to meet Jesus. Jesus' disciples came with him too.

Imagine what the party must have been like. It's about real people! I sense a lively, animated, if not boisterous atmosphere filled with laughter. It is not somber at all! I imagine curiosity about Jesus, and at the same time a playful spirit of camaraderie. Jesus is there, not in a corner, somber, but engaged meeting Matthew's friends. It was in these environments that Jesus genuinely connected with people, and some wisdom from on High couldn't help but come out in the conversations.

Wine was served at banquets, as we later see at the wedding feast in Cana with Jesus in attendance. I see Jesus enjoying wine with the tax collectors, the others, and his followers in the midst of conversations. Conversations that, I'm sure, were mesmerizing. Thought-provoking. Challenging. Piercing. Delightful. Encouraging. Hopeful. Convincing. Loving. Awe-filled. Drinking wine. Life-changing conversations filled the house.

A banquet like this wasn't going to happen at the synagogue. Why?

First, the religious leaders—the Pharisees—would not permit the unclean rift-raft in the synagogue. They were not welcome.

Secondly, the synagogue was neither a place of freedom of expression, nor a place to question religion—only a place where formal correspondence to tediously defined rites and acts made one "holy."

Thirdly, no tax collector or other sinners were going to show up at a synagogue, only to be judged and condemned.

But at Matthew's house, his friends were comfortable, safe, and free to be themselves. And Jesus later told the Pharisees, that these were the people with whom he came to associate and serve.

As the Pharisees did get wind of the party at Matthew's house, they were not happy about it! They have previously accused Jesus of being a drunkard and a glutton, so Jesus' attendance at Matthew's banquet was further evidence—drinking wine and breaking bread with sinners and tax collectors!

The Pharisees and the teachers of the law who belonged to their sect complained to his disciples. "Why do you eat and drink with tax collectors and sinners?" they asked according to Luke 5:30. In this instance, even some of John the Baptist's disciples raised the same question as the Pharisees. "They (Pharisees) said to him, 'John's disciples often fast and pray, and so do the disciples of the Pharisees, but yours go on eating and drinking,'" (Luke 5:33).

Jesus answered, "Can you make the guests of the bridegroom fast while he is with them? The time for feasting, enjoying, and celebrating is now, while Jesus is with the people! Jesus was saying that the gathering at Matthew's house had all the meaning of a wedding feast: That he was the bridegroom, and all those tax collectors and sinners were the invited guests to the wedding feast. The opposition and the accusation of the Pharisees was not going to dampen this festive gathering.

Jesus Teaches From Wine

Jesus took the opportunity to give some spiritual guidance after this encounter with the Pharisees criticism of Matthew's party. He turned to wine to illustrate.

"You cannot put new wine in old wineskins." New wine is in a volatile state of fermentation—foaming, expanding, and stretching. Old wineskins are stiff and have lost elasticity and cannot expand with the action of the new wine. The old wineskin will burst under the pressure. New wine must be put in a new wineskin.

Jesus made the point that the Pharisees' legalistic demands—that all must do like them to be "righteous"— is an old story. Jesus is saying, "I've come with a new story." The Pharisee's story hasn't worked, and that story like an old wineskin, could not possibly hold the new wine of a whole new way of thinking and living that includes freedom, forgiveness, prosperity of life, and grace. The latter was new wine, and the old wineskin of the Pharisee's way was inadequate!

The banquet going on at Matthew's house with Jesus and his disciples in attendance was part of that new wine's expression, and it was nothing like the religiosity of the Pharisees—a way that only sees the external form and structure and not the heart.

Jesus' consistent message is that we are made new inside. Inside is where you find true change and abundant life. It's new wine!

In Luke's Gospel, there's a second, important wine illustration. "And no one after drinking old wine wants the new, for he says, 'The old is better,'" Luke 5:38. There is a bit of a twist here, as it seems to contradict—that old wine is better than the new, but Jesus was using another comparison the Pharisees would be familiar.

He was simply saying to them, "The new wine is better! You Pharisees should not take your old religious customs, traditions, forms and structures too seriously—they're old wine." The Pharisee did not want the new wine that represented the new way Jesus was offering. It attacked their pride, threatening their perceived self-importance, religious superiority, their power and control that they forced over everyone.

Through wine, Jesus taught about true religion, true spirituality, and the new relationship with God. If, as some say, wine is evil, it is hard to conceive that Jesus would use it to represent true spirituality. Wine is a special and beautiful symbol of the Gospel—the good news!

This good news of Jesus, The Christ, is new wine for the soul. Because the Gospel is the good news, Jesus chose the metaphor of wine to symbolize it. We are not to gaze at the wine of the Gospel. We are to participate in it by enjoying it. The wine must be savored.

Just as wine is drunk heartily as God's gift, so the new life that Jesus came to demonstrate is to be absorbed and enjoyed as God's gift. And as wine refreshes, so communion with Jesus refreshes our souls. There is no error in God's sovereign choice of wine as a metaphor for the Gospel. Jesus invites us to his table to drink the wine of new life.

Blushing Waters—The Miracle At Cana

The conscious water saw its master, and blushed.[11]

A wedding is one of the most significant events in Jewish culture and a cause for jubilant celebration. It was true at the time of Jesus, and true today in Jewish life. The wedding at Cana was typical. In those days, the wedding and what we would call the reception was a full-blown event lasting up to a week. There was a constant stream of guests arriving and departing throughout the week. The guests enjoyed the festivities and celebration for the new couple joined in marriage. It was customary for the host to provide wine for the guests. But this wedding party at Cana ran into a problem. Somehow, Mary, the mother of Jesus, became aware of the circumstance.

"They have no more wine," Mary told Jesus. This was a big deal, and would be extremely embarrassing. This social snafu could bring disgrace to the bridegroom and the family for years to come.

In English translations of the Bible, it is easy to miss the nuances of the text because we are not familiar with the idioms of the original language. On the surface the response of Jesus to Mary might seem rude and disrespectful, but in the idiom of the day, here is the tone and demeanor of that conversation.

Mary came to Jesus with the problem, she obviously expected Him to do something; His respectful response was something like this, "Dear woman, I will handle this my way. I have a plan different from yours." Jesus' comment that "My time has not yet come," means that it was not time for him to go public revealing himself as the Messiah. Mary understood what Jesus was saying, and she told the attendants to do as Jesus instructed. Mary's response doesn't blow Jesus' cover that "his time has not yet come." Mary had confidence and trusted in what Jesus would do. She knew he would do something, and it would be the right thing.

Jesus told the attendants to fill six stone pots with water. The stone pots were provided for the guests for ceremonial cleansing in obedience to the religious practices prescribed by the spiritual leaders—the Pharisees—the party poopers.

The attendants got carried away with the task and filled all the pots to the brim, so that there was no room for anything else like some added magic ingredient. The only explanation for the water changing into wine was that Jesus by his power did it! It required no added ingredient, no slight of hand, and no gimmick. He just did it. When he told the attendants to draw some out and take it to the banquet master, they saw "the conscious water blush" becoming wine!

Jesus showed sensitivity and sympathy to the potentially embarrassing social situation for the bridegroom and his family, and responded with his first miracle—changing water into wine. Jesus kept this miracle low key, and quiet. So did the disciples. The story of this miracle was recorded in only one gospel. Other than the attendants who drew the water, no one at the party knew the source of the wine, at least not right away. When the wine was presented to the banquet master and he tasted it, he pulled the bridegroom aside and said, "Everyone brings out the choice wine first, and then the cheaper wine after the guests have had too much to drink; but you have saved the best till now." The banquet master was amazed by the gesture. It was a most extraordinary gesture that no doubt caught the attention of the guests.

There is another interesting nuance to the scene— the rich imagery of the stone pots. The six stone pots, which Jesus chose for the attendants to fill with water, were the pots used by the Jews for "ceremonial washing,"—the custom of purification. Each pot held around 25 to 30 gallons. The fact that there were six pots holding that much water tells us just how significant ceremonial cleansing was in religious and social life—and in the Jewish culture there is no dichotomy dividing life into separated compartments such as secular and spiritual.

The instructions and rites of ceremonial cleansing were elaborate. The longest part of the Mishnah was devoted to instructions on proper and ceremonial purification and cleansing, and the section about cleaning hands covers many chapters. (The Mishnah is part of the Talmud—the official document interpreting the Jewish religion and prescribing its various practices. It reached its full development around 500 CE.)

Again, the Pharisees believed they had to be ritually clean by performing all sorts of specific ritual ceremonial cleaning. This was their way of showing their "spirituality," their appearance of holiness, and their acceptance by God. These same religious leaders really believed that association with the wrong people would contaminate them, even by touching something "those" people had touched. Remember the response of the Pharisees when they saw Jesus associating with the tax collectors at Levi's house.

By choosing the six water pots reserved for ceremonial cleansing, Jesus made an important spiritual statement. With the ceremonial washing pots now filled with wine, Jesus eliminated the possibility that anyone at the wedding feast could engage in further ceremonial cleansing acts of purification! This tangible external form of spiritual purity of the Pharisees was replaced by what only Jesus could provide. Pots filled with wine! With one miracle, Jesus rejected the superficial, self-righteous practice of purification and replaced that symbol with a picture of his gift of authentic purity and spirituality. Jesus filled the pots with his gift of the finest wine, a symbol of the "abundant life" He came to give—and you don't even have to clean up before you drink the gift!

Jesus replaced self-righteous, superficial, hypocritical practices of purification, and said, "Come to me, sit at the lavish table I have prepared for you; drink from my banquet table of fine aged wine like that described in Isaiah 25:6-8." You can empty your pots for cleaning yourself up, and let Jesus fill your pot with the best wine. That's good news!

The Last Supper

It was not just any supper; it was the last supper Jesus would have with his disciples. The supper is described in Matthew 26:26-30, in Marks's Gospel in 14:22-26, and Luke 22:7-20.

In keeping with custom, Jesus made preparation to keep the Passover with the disciples. Jesus was in the last days of his three-year ministry on earth that will soon lead to the cross.

The Last Supper has captured the attention of artists, scholars, and spiritual pilgrims throughout the ages. The Last

Supper inaugurates one of the most important sacraments and symbols of the Christian faith, and shows Jesus' obedience to the Jewish celebration of Passover. The Last Supper inspires artists to capture this moment in antiquity, and nurtures and awakens the spirit of believers helping them remember and appreciate their relationship to Jesus, the Christ.

The Last Supper is about Jesus' fulfillment of his earthly ministry and provides the background for his final time with all the disciples together. It is in this setting that Jesus elevates the cup of wine to a new level as a divine symbol.

The Passover in the time of Jesus was opened with a two-part blessing—one for the day, and one for the food. Jesus followed tradition with the blessing saying to His disciples, "I have eagerly desired to eat this Passover with you before I suffer." That is the first blessing. After the first blessing (Luke 22:14), Jesus pronounced the second blessing on the food saying: "For I tell you, I will not eat it again, until it finds fulfillment in the Kingdom of God." After taking the cup, he gave thanks and said, "Take this and divide it among you. For I tell you, I will not drink again of the fruit of the vine with you until The kingdom of God comes."

Then Jesus passed the first cup of wine, as is the custom of the Passover. The cup of wine is drunk four times during the Passover. That practice comes from the Old Testament book of Exodus in verses 6:6-7. Layered in meaning to Jews and Christians alike, the Last Supper looks back to the deliverance of the Jews from slavery from the Egyptians, and for Christians, the deliverance from the bondage of the kingdom of darkness into the kingdom of light. It is the third cup—that of redemption— that is core to the Christian's spiritual experience: The Cup of Redemption.

The four cups of wine stand for the four "I wills" of Exodus 6:6-7:

> *The Cup of Sanctification: "I will bring you out from under the burdens of the Egyptians."*

The Cup of Judgment: "I will rid you out of their bondage."
The Cup of Redemption: "I will redeem you with an outstretched arm"
The Cup of Praise: "I will take you to me for a people."

The beauty and meaning of the Seder Service or Sacrament of the Lord's Supper enlightens us with greater insight and understanding of the spiritual refreshment symbolized in the cup of wine. In the light of the Passover we learn:

Wine is the cup drunk to celebrate the Passover, and wine continually appears in spiritual practices in the Bible.

It is the third cup of the Passover that Jesus drank with his disciples with these words: "Drink from it, all of you. This is my blood of the covenant, which is poured out for many for the forgiveness of sins." When Christians observe the Lord's Supper or Communion, they are taking the third cup of the Passover—the cup of redemption. It is in the imagery of the Last Supper that Christian faith finds itself cradled in the rich history and practice of our Jewish brothers and sisters.

As the supper is drawing to a close, Jesus said to his disciples, as recorded in Matthew's Gospel chapter 26, verse 29, "But I say to you, I will not drink of this fruit of the vine from now on until that day when I drink it new with you in My Father's Kingdom." By saying "drink again" Jesus affirmed that he drank wine, and these words only make sense if Jesus has drunk wine before.

Another key phrase is "when I drink it new with you." Here Jesus was referring to drinking alone on the cross, but shortly after the cross, he will drink wine again with others in the kingdom. Some believe when Jesus will drink again in the Kingdom is far into a future not yet realized, but Jesus frequently told his audiences that the "kingdom is at hand!" That means the Kingdom is here and now, not in the future. Acts 10:40-41 then tells that Jesus is eating and drinking with others (in the present Kingdom) shortly after his resurrection!

And Jesus, once again, answering the Pharisees, explained where the Kingdom was located: "The kingdom is within you."

Once, having been asked by the Pharisees when the kingdom of God would come, Jesus replied, "The kingdom of God does not come with your careful observation, nor will people say, 'Here it is,' or 'There it is,' because the kingdom of God is within you."

Summarizing, Jesus explained that the Kingdom is now, and the Kingdom is within you. I will drink alone on the cross. I drink wine with you now! I will drink wine with you again shortly.

In the Passover and the Lord's Supper, wine is an integral part of one of the most sacred spiritual expressions of Jewish and Christian faith.

The New Testament and the words and practice of Jesus affirm the divine permission to drink and enjoy wine. The permission reveals itself in the natural reading and normative understanding revealed in the context and interpretation of the words and events.

If wine is intrinsically bad and a divine prohibition, it would be a contradiction of the highest magnitude that Jesus and God the Father would choose wine as a core symbol of the Gospel—good news!

The beauty of wine's symbolism of the Gospel—good news, and all that it represents in the Divine Economy is reason to celebrate the Divine Permission to enjoy wine! Drinking wine is a "remembering" of Jesus. Each time a follower of Jesus drinks wine, it is a remembering of Jesus regardless of occasion. Drink your wine and remember.

"It Is Finished!"

Jesus drank wine alone on the cross. He had said to his disciples at the Passover supper they shared together, that, "I will not drink wine again with you until we drink it together in My Father's Kingdom."

For some time, I did not understand the offering of two wines to Jesus on the cross. He did not take the first wine, but He drank the second. Jim West, writing in *Drinking With Calvin And Luther* explains the two wines:

> *The first he refused, it being a drug that would deaden his pain and make him less conscious of his redeeming work. But the sour wine or vinegar was received by Christ. According to Eerdman's* The New Bible Dictionary, *the posca of the Romans was an acidic wine and formed part of the soldiers rations. "It is this which was offered to the crucified Christ as refreshment (Mark 15:36; John 19:29, 30), and was different from the myrrh flavored anodyne which he had refused earlier (Matthew 27:34; Mark 15:23)."*[12]

The first wine was a hallucinogenic. Wine mixed with myrrh was known to be such—you could say it was a drug of the day. Jesus refused the wine knowing it would rob him of his consciousness.

This second wine from a Roman soldier's rations, gave refreshment to the suffering Christ. After taking this wine, Jesus is refreshed and animated, and declared those triumphant words, "It is finished!" West says,

> *This is not a perfunctory report about finishing a drink. On the contrary, being fortified and refreshed by the wine, he was enabled to shout victoriously... "It is finished." His "it is finished" was not his final whimper, but the shout of the mighty man who shouts by reason of wine...*[13]

Throughout the Bible and other historical sources, wine is mentioned as a tonic used to refresh, animate, and elevate soldiers. It is fitting that wine serves that purpose at Jesus' moment of triumph.

Redemption is wine-soaked. The third cup of wine at the Passover is the cup of redemption. Jesus offered this third cup of wine—the cup of redemption—and told the disciples to drink all of it. At the cross, wine was given that animates and refreshes Jesus. Energized, Jesus declared, "It is finished."

The Question Of Diluted Wine

Many believe the wine of Jesus' time was wine diluted with water—according to some rabbinic traditions—one part wine to three parts water, or two parts wine to one part water.

Wine in the Old Testament was undiluted. Diluted wine was considered to be a bad thing. In fact, diluted wine was viewed as a dishonest practice. References to mixed wine in the Old Testament refer to wine mixed with other spices, and maybe other fruits. (See Chapter 3 for a description of mixed wines.)

At the closing of the time period covered by the Old Testament (around 400 BCE), wine for sacrifices and regular consumption is undiluted, and acceptable for offerings and sacrifices. By the time we come to Jesus, some sources indicate that wine used for sacrifices and offerings was diluted with water. This would represent a deterioration of spiritual practice rather than advancement.

Old Testament offerings and sacrifices called for unblemished lambs, new undiluted wine, and first fruits of produce, for example, for offerings and sacrifices. However, by the time of Jesus, diluted wine was in use, because religion and culture had changed.

The issue of diluted wine is insignificant to the divine permission to drink wine, and there is not an instruction that one should only drink wine mixed with water.

What Would Jesus Drink?

Jesus participated and co-mingled in everyday life, with everyday people, enjoying their celebrations, family life, and other social engagements. Jesus' attendance at Matthew's party where he ate and drank with tax collectors and sinners, and the Cana wedding feast, where he performed his first miracle by changing water into wine testify to his participation and approval of the social customs. He participated in Passover, drinking wine with his disciples—establishing wine as a symbol of a new covenant of grace for all.

Jesus ate the diet of the day, drank wine, and even drank wine with social rejects. He did so responsibly, and by his behavior approved the moderate consumption of wine, giving us a model to celebrate and enjoy in life.

CHAPTER 6

WINE IN THE FIFTH GOSPEL:

The Holy Land

The land of Israel staggers beneath its burden of history and myth, and much of that intoxicating scripturally sanctified baggage is wine-sodden.[14]

A Land Like No Other

The land of Israel is known to Jews and Christians today as The Holy Land. The land of Palestine is the sacred soil on which God established his covenant and relationship with his chosen people the Jews. It is the land that gave birth to Jesus and the Christian faith.

Many describe the land, called Palestine in the Bible, as The Fifth Gospel, because the land itself is the birthplace of the Hebrew culture, the Jewish religion, and the life and times of Jesus Christ. The land is the place where Christianity begins. In my world travels, I find no land like the Holy Land. It is a land steeped in religious history, a land that testifies of God's interaction with humanity, and a land that beckons spiritual pilgrims to come. It is a mysterious land in many ways as the setting of the old covenant story. It is a land that has seen the best and worst of the human drama. It is a land that has seen the blessing of God's abundance. It is a land that has seen barrenness, and seen God turn away as its people abandoned God, justice, and truth.

The land hosts the magnificent city of Jerusalem, where all three monotheistic religions have holy sites. When spiritual pilgrims first enter Jerusalem and come to the Mount of Olives and view the breath-taking panorama of Jerusalem for the first time, most are silenced. Hearts are deeply touched as one reflects on the breadth and depth of spiritual history played out in the city.

The Holy Land and the City of Jerusalem today are at the center of conflict and brokenness as strife between Israelis and Palestinians, Jew and Arab, corrupt the land. Yet, in spite of all its challenges, Israel is once again a land of milk and honey, and of plentiful wine. And may it soon be a land of peace and harmony.

I've enjoyed meals and wine with Palestinian Christians in Bethlehem, and I have sat at tables with Jewish brothers and sisters enjoying the fruit of the vine and the bounty of the land —this land of wine and spirit. The land of Palestine can boast of a long and rich wine history. Almost everywhere the land tells us about wine. From gold goblets for drinking wine unearthed in archaeological digs to the remains of ancient wine presses, the land tells a story of the importance and value of wine in biblical culture from the first recorded history of wine in the story of Noah to the time of Jesus.

Wine In Ancient Israel

Again, Andrew Jafford writes in *The Evening Standard Wine Guide 1997*:

> *What Christian would not want to drink the wine of Cana or Galilee after a thoughtful afternoon amongst the splintered, fissured olives of Gethsemane. What Jew would prefer a French kosher wine to one from the land which Moses' spies returned bearing an enormous cluster of grapes suspended from a pole?*[15]

For more than 5000 years, the vine and the wine have featured prominently in the relationship of the people to one another, and most prominently in the relationship between

God and his people. As we recounted earlier, the first recorded history of wine is the story of Noah planting a vineyard after the great flood. From Noah onward, wine was integral to the history of the land and people of Palestine, modern day Israel.

In Deuteronomy 7:12-13, God's provision of blessing is described:

> If you will pay attention to these laws and are faithful to follow then the Lord your God will keep His covenant of love with you, as He swore to your forefathers. He will love you and bless you and increase your numbers. He will bless the fruit of your womb, the crops of your land—your grain, new wine, and oil...

I emphasize the words love and bless because that is what God desired for the people of Israel. Sixteen times the Bible mentions grain, wine, and oil as the top produce of the land—the chief blessing of the soil. Wine was always a blessing from God to his people! Not only that, wine, grain, and oil were the base of the economy of the country, and a measure of God's favor.

Another Old Testament text, Deuteronomy 8:6-8, 10 repeats the blessing of the land God intended for the people:

> Observe the commands of the Lord your God and walking in His ways and revering Him. For the Lord your God is bringing you into a good land—a land with streams and pools of water, with springs flowing in the valleys and hills; a land with wheat and barley, vines and fig trees, pomegranates, olive oil and honey... When you have eaten and are satisfied, praise the Lord your God for the good land He has given you.

The vine is one of the fruits by which the land was blessed. In the Torah, (the first five books of the Old Testament), the book of Deuteronomy is a review or a rehearsal of God's covenant or agreement with his people—what was required of them, and the consequent blessing God had in store for them.

All of the prophets of Israel used the vine as a symbol of the happy state God provided for the people. Ezekiel 17:1-10 and 19:10-14 regard the vine as a symbol of the people of Israel. The vine and wine were used prominently in the language of love and blessing God has for his people. There were laments, as well, regarding the blessing of the vine being withheld because of Israel's unfaithfulness to God.

In good times, when Israel was faithful to the Lord, the land brought forth abundant fruit of the vine, new wine flourished, and there was jubilation. When Israel was unfaithful, the vine gave bad fruit or withered away and the joy and the blessing of wine was withheld. In those times there was great sorrow and sadness, and any shouts were from anguish, because wine was so valued and such a significant measure of God's blessing.

The remains of thousands of wine presses dot the landscape of Israel, and remain as a testament of the importance of wine in Palestine's history, and the presses stand as a reminder of repeated blessings at the pressing floor.

Another beautiful picture is described in Isaiah 5:1-2. In this poetic verse the prophet likens God to the vineyard owner and Israel as the vineyard. In poetic verse, a detailed description of how to plant a vineyard was described:

> I will sing for the one I love
> a song about his vineyard:
> My loved one had a vineyard
> on a fertile hillside.
> He dug it up and cleared it of stones
> and planted it with choice vines.
> He built a watchtower in it
> and cut out a winepress as well.

While the verse is about God's relationship to his people, the description tells about agricultural practices. The description of the steps of planting the vineyard are good agricultural practice in planting and tending a vineyard, like locating vineyards at higher elevations for greater temperature changes between day and night. The cooler nights cause the fruit to ripen more slowly adding to the sugar content that produces higher quality grapes, and higher quality wines.

Throughout the history of Israel, there were cycles of blessing and shouts of joy at the abundance of wine as Israel lived in faithfulness to God, and there were eras of blessing withheld, the fruit of the vine withheld, and sorrow, sadness, and distress filled the land when there was no wine.

Daniel Rogov is Israel's most respected and influential wine critic today. Each year he publishes *Rogov's Guide To Israeli Wines* rating wines and wineries. In the guide, he recounts another era of Israel's history, the times of the First and Second Temples. Rogov states, "...wine was widely consumed by the local populace, but the very best were set aside for libations in the Temple."[16]

The Temple was the center of religious life in Israel. The sacrificial system of offerings required the very best be offered to God, including the very best of wine. Among the requirements: a quarter of a hin (about 1.5 gallons) of wine with a lamb; a third of a hin (about 2 gallons) for a ram offered; a half hin (about 3 gallons)for a bull offered.

The people were required to give a tithe of their new wine to the Temple (Deuteronomy 12:17). Rogov further describes the importance and value placed on wine:

> *Wines were so central to the culture during the days of the first and second Temples that those who planted vineyards were exempt from military service! Illustrations of grapes, grape leaves, amphorae (wine containers), and drinking vessels were often used as symbols on seals and coins as well as for decorations on the friezes of buildings.*[17]

Wine is an integral part of Jewish religious rites and ceremonies. Wine binds and fuses Israel, Judaism, the Jewish people, and the Holy Land into a unique association. This association then crosses into Christianity as it is uniquely fused to Israel, Judaism, the Jewish people, and the Holy Land.

The land of the fifth gospel produced wine when Jesus lived and walked there. Wines were known for place and style then—the lighter wines of Sharon and the stronger wines of Carmel for example. The land also gave fruit wines of dates, apples, and other fruits. Wines were still imported from Italy, Greece, and Lebanon in spite of the abundance and quality of local wines. The wine trade was thriving in the land during Jesus' life. Greek amphorae have been discovered throughout Israel giving evidence of significant importation of wines from Greece. Yet, the fifth gospel yielded its fruit in local wines of style and quality. Jesus knew the land of wine and spirit. It raises the question again, "What kind of wine did Jesus' miracle at Cana produce? Maybe, one day we will know.

The Holy Land continued to be a wine culture for thousands of years, and from the time of Jesus to the seventh century, the Holy Land produced wines of such high quality that they were sought after by the Romans and shipped to their military throughout the Mediterranean and North Africa.

The Holy Land abruptly ceased to be a wine-growing region with the Muslim conquest in 636 CE, and remained dormant until the nineteenth century when new Jewish settlement renewed local winemaking.

New Wine

The new wines from Israel from the nineteenth century were not the best, and were produced primarily for ceremonial purposes. It took time for the wines of Israel to achieve the level of quality to be described as world quality wines.

That change came in the early 1980s when Israel's modern wine industry experienced a rebirth—centered around the first releases of Golan Height's Winery in 1984.

A new chapter of Israeli wines began to be written. The quality of Golan Heights Winery's wines altered the perception that wines from Israel were the heavy, red, sweet wines produced for religious purposes.

Golan Heights Winery proved that quality varietal wines could be produced in Israel. Other wineries followed producing quality wines worthy of international recognition. Today there are at least five major wineries, 12 medium-sized wineries, and many small boutique wineries in Israel producing high-quality, world class wines.[18]

The Fifth Gospel, The Holy Land, is once again a land of abundant good wine! The Holy Land is once again a land of wine and spirit!

CHAPTER 7

DRINKING WITH DOM, MARTIN, AND JOHN

It has become quite a common proverb that in wine, there is truth. (Pliny the Elder, 23-79)

After the time period of the biblical narrative, the next 2000 years sees the church as the dominant and pervasive institution influencing and controlling cultures, governments, personal thinking, attitudes, and practice. Few societies escaped the influence of the church. Through edicts, counsels, declarations, and proclamations, the church defined truth for the world, taught how to worship, and dictated how to be right with God. The impact of the church, I'm afraid, is a mixed bag.

Wine and wine drinking did not escape the sharp eye of the church, and the church's historical influence and impact on wine may be surprising to some. That wine is a gift of God to be appreciated and enjoyed is established in the biblical record itself, and church leaders continued to affirm this view about wine.

A sample survey of Christian scholars and church leaders throughout the history of the church finds affirmation that wine is a gift from God to be enjoyed. The following are some of the voices of the church speaking about wine—voices from some well-known, and-not-so-well-known church leaders.

Dom Pérignon

Who has not heard the famous name of perhaps the most prestigious name in Champagne, Dom Pérignon? Dom Pérignon is considered by many to be the benchmark of quality Champagne, and there is a man behind the name.

There are many larger-than-life stories and legends told about Pérignon including the famous line, "I'm drinking stars," he reportedly exclaimed on tasting the bubbly the first time. Whether he said it or not, or whether the many stories told of him are true, he certainly deserves recognition as the "patron saint" of Champagne.

You may not associate wine with the church, much less use the two words in the same sentence. But who would even think to ask what the church has to do with the "bubbly?"

Throughout history, the church and church leaders have acted as the custodians of wine! The church is associated with advancements, and developments in winemaking from vineyard management to the winemaking process. The church and wine are continuously linked in history, and one can wonder what might have happened to wine were it not for the church.

Dom Pérignon is a case in point. As a Benedictine monk, he develops Champagne in a church institution! So, drinking a glass of Champagne or a sparkling wine, is to enjoy the fruit and labor of the church!

Dom Pierre Pérignon was born in 1640 in Saint-Menehould, east of the Champagne region. Pérignon was schooled in advanced theological studies from age 18 and became a Benedictine monk chosing a life of celibacy and communion with God.

At age 19, he entered the Benedictine Order at the Abbey of Saint-Vannes at Verdun. At age 28, he was appointed the cellarmaster at the Abbey of Hautvillers. Pérignon is often credited with the discovery of Champagne. However, most agree the sparkling was created earlier. But, there is no doubt that Dom Pérignon is the father of Champagne, as he put Champagne on the world's wine map and elevated the making of Champagne to an art.

He apparently possessed a heightened sense of taste. He followed the same process each year. A week or so before harvest, bunches of grapes picked from individual sections of the 40-acre estate would be put on the windowsill overnight to cool. The next morning he would begin tasting the grapes on an empty stomach. He was then able to blend the grapes— deciding which grapes from what parcels of the estate, and in what proportion, would come up with the best blend to make the Champagne. This was a remarkable feat of blending!

`Per-Henrik Mansson and Ted Loos writing in *Wine Spectator* conclude, "Dom Pérignon created the legendary 'vin de Pérignon.' His blanc de noirs, a white bubbly made with red grapes, became the first outstanding sparkling wine and changed the history of Champagne."[19] I bet you haven't read that in a church history text!

In the 1920s, Champagne Moet et Chandon adopted Pérignon's name for their prestige blend of Champagne. It continues to be a prestige Champagne.

Dom Pérignon, theologian, churchman, cellarmaster, and father of Champagne, has earned his place in the Christian Hall of Wine Fame. With your next glass of Champagne or sparkling wine, pause, and give thanks to God, and give thanks for Dom Pérignon!

Martin Luther

I remember reading the sign on the doorway of a monastery in Paris some years ago: "Our brothers and sisters in rebellion are welcome." I had to think for a moment, and then I realized that they were speaking of me. I am a Protestant of sorts. Although I think the protesting ended long ago, when it comes to Martin Luther, it depends on what side of the Catholic and Protestant divide you fall. For me, Martin Luther is a hero of faith and has a rightful place in the Christian Hall of Fame because of his enjoyment of beer and wine.

What a character—courageous, outspoken, but with an infectious sense of humor, Luther enjoyed beer and wine. He wrote, "Beer is made by man, wine by God!" Most students of

Luther think he had a preference for beer, but he surely enjoyed wine as well.

When he married Katie, the city of Wittenberg gave them a cellar of beer and wine as a wedding gift. In a letter to Katie he once wrote, "You must wonder how long I am likely to be gone or, rather how long you will be rid of me. I keep thinking what good wine and beer I have at home, as well as a beautiful wife, or shall I say Lord?"

By all accounts, the reformer Luther enjoyed wine and beer as a part of everyday life. He had a mug with three rings. One represented the Lord's Prayer, one the Ten Commandments, and the other the Apostle's Creed. Luther could drink to the last ring, the Lord's Prayer, but a friend of his could never make it past the Ten Commandments.

Luther was passionate that Communion be taken with wine preferring that the sacrament be eliminated rather than replace wine for the sacrament!

A faithful servant of the Lord, a theologian of historic magnitude—the leader of the great Reformation, Luther appreciated the good gifts of God, namely good beer and wine.

John Calvin

Having studied the theological works of Calvin in a purely intellectual vein, I thought of him as straight-laced, a prude, and lacking any sense of humor. I was first introduced to the following statement by Calvin in *Drinking With Calvin And Luther* by Jim West:

> *We are no where forbidden to laugh, or to be satisfied with food, or to annex new possessions to those already enjoyed by ourselves or our ancestors, or to be delighted with music, or to drink wine....*[20]

I always admired Calvin's intellectual stature, and appreciated his commentaries on the Scriptures and other theological writings. I had formed an image of Calvin as a that impersonal, matter-of-fact intellectual, but this comment in the Institutes spurred me on to discover the man, John Calvin, and my perception proved to be wrong.

West in his book highlights another quote from Calvin, "It is permissible to use wine not only for necessity, but to make us merry." In Calvin's commentary on Psalm 104:15, he warned against making the peril of drunkenness "a pretext...for a new cult based upon abstinence."[21]

Calvin enjoyed wine, and by all historical accounts, valued wine as a gift from God, and commended drinking wine asserting that those who enjoy wine "feel a livelier gratitude to God."

John Wesley

The following is an entry from Wesley's journal. The remarkable entry is from July 6, 1746:

> *We agreed it would prevent great expense, as well as of health as of time and money, if the poorer people of our society could be persuaded to leave off drinking tea. We resolved ourselves to begin and set the example...*[22]

It appears that this is where the term "teetotaler" originates. It is one who abstains from tea! Tea was a costly commodity and a burden on the meager wages of working people, so Wesley decided to set an example by abstaining from tea that hopefully would help workers abstain and save money.

He did not do this with other beverages. Wesley viewed beer and ale as healthier than tea! In English society and Methodist circles, drinking wine, beer, and ale was a part of Christian practice.

George Whitefield

George Whitefield is regarded as one of the greatest evangelist in the history of the church. Growing up, his parents owned an inn where he worked in his youth serving drinks (what we call a bartender) during the day, and wrote sermons at night. Whitefield enjoyed wine, beer, and ale. In a letter he writes, "Give my thanks to that friendly brewer for the keg of rum he sent." Pastors in early America were often paid in rum and other drink!

Charles Spurgeon

The biographies of Charles Spurgeon tell us he enjoyed wine, beer, and brandy, which he drank to the glory of God. Spurgeon had a keen sense of humor, and also enjoyed smoking cigars. The story is told that he once commented to another pastor that if he ever smoked to excess he would quit. When asked what would he consider to be excess he replied, "Why, smoking two cigars at the same time." Spurgeon practiced moderation in all things!

J. Gresham Machen

J. Gresham Machen The founder of Westminster Seminary in Philadelphia, voted "no" on a resolution to endorse the 18th Amendment and the Volstead Act. Because of this vote, he was labeled as sympathetic to drunkenness, and further slandered by Christians who called him a drunk. A rumor spread that he also received his income from breweries. Machen was discredited by fellow Christians over this vote completely ignoring his consistent character and testimony as a theologian and a devout follower of Jesus.

The Puritans

Jim West reports this story about the Puritans. The Puritans sailed to America in 1630. One of their ships, the Arabella carried 42 tons of beer and 10,000 gallons of wine, almost forgetting to load fresh water![23]

Elijah Craig

While not directly related to wine, Elijah Craig was a Baptist minister that many believe was the first to distill bourbon whiskey in America in 1789! That assertion is discredited by history, but the legend persists that he was the first to distill bourbon. But for certain, Craig, the Baptist minister, was a master distiller of bourbon whiskey!

A New History

These anecdotes are but a few examples of Christian leaders who upheld an appreciation of wine, beer, and other alcoholic beverages consumed in moderation. The short accounts above demonstrate through the ages, that wine drinking among Christians was common. The modernist view, that of abstinence or prohibition of alcohol, is an exception to the history and practice of the church when it comes to drinking wine (and other alcohol) in moderation. Remember John Calvin's warning that we not take the peril of drunkenness as "a pretext for a cult of abstinence."

The development of wine and the institution of religion, Jewish and Christian, Catholic or Protestant—are inextricably woven together. The church and wine are inseparable. God gave wine. The church preserved and developed the gift!

Wine historian Hugh Johnson aptly sums up the relationship of the church with wine:

> *The links between wine and worship, whether through the ancient gods, the Jewish and Christian rites, or the initiatives of monasteries and bishops, recur so often in our story that the storyteller must keep challenging himself: was it really religion that called the tune again?*[24]

CHAPTER 8

A TOAST TO SPIRIT!

What A Glass Of Wine Can Do
For Your Spirit

Give beer to those who are perishing, wine to those in anguish; let them drink and forget their poverty and remember their misery no more. (Proverbs 31:6-7)

"What can a glass of wine do for your spirit—your soul?" Is wine good for your emotional and mental health? I propose, that not only is wine good for the individual, it is good for community. Wine is a drink of social interaction. In looking at the effect of wine on the emotional, spiritual, and mental well-being of the individual, it is important to see, as we often see in the biblical texts, wine is best enjoyed in the company of others. People who enjoy wine would much rather enjoy that glass of wine with friends, family, and their relational community. Wine is just that way—a beverage you talk about with others.

People in all sorts of communities, friends from work, church or spiritual community, and family, enjoy wine more when the experience is shared with others. People enjoy being with other people with whom they share a common spirit. Community, by its nature is spiritual, whether it's a religious group, a band of friends at a local bar, or neighbors gathered for a backyard barbecue.

All around the world—in pubs, restaurants, and other public houses—it is refreshing to see people coming together in community, radiating a light spirit of camaraderie as they share together a meal, conversation, laughter, and wine. These shared moments of community provide many significant "all is well" times in our lives.

Hugh Johnson, in the opening words of his classic history of wine, *Vintage*, says with forthright clarity:

> *It was not the subtle bouquet of wine, or a lingering aftertaste of violets and raspberries, that first caught the attention of our ancestors. It was, I'm afraid its effect.*[25]

Johnson further says of our early ancestors that life was "nasty, brutish, and short; those who first felt the effects of alcohol believed they were being given a preview of paradise."

Our enjoyment and appreciation of wine would be greatly diminished were it not for the "effect." Wine is a complete package—a drink made from the grapes of the vine and given its special character by the process of fermentation where sugar and yeast come together and produce alcohol. So, we experience the color, taste, smell, and texture of the grapes, and we experience wine's effect from the alcohol. All this together is the wine experience, and the experience doesn't escape the notice of God. A frequent biblical comment on wine is the mention of wine's effect of "elevating" our spirit. More on this later in the chapter.

In the shadow of American history, prohibition distorts the reality that alcohol, wine especially, possesses any virtue. The era of American history that produced the prohibitionists movement and ultimately the Amendment to the Constitution prohibiting the manufacture and sale of alcoholic beverages, is a rather perplexing chapter in our history. It was indeed a time of its own "nasty, brutish" character coming at a time of migration from the rural countryside to cities. There was a great deal of drinking and drunkenness. Was the excessive use of alcohol that out of the ordinary? I think it is hard to say.

It is beyond our scope here to attempt to explain all the social, religious, and political complexities that led to prohibition, but history has shown that prohibition is not an effective deterrent to abuse. As a matter of fact, alcohol consumption in the United States increased during prohibition.[26] Ultimately, the best government, the best law, is self-discipline by the individual.

In order to survive and flourish, societies must have laws that provide for rule and order. But history attests that you cannot take this to an extreme and try to order the detailed behavior of the individual. If you are interested in examining the phenomena of prohibition, an outstanding book is *LAST CALL: The Rise and Fall Of Prohibition by Daniel Okrent*, (Scribner).[27]

The Bible isn't silent about the "effect" of wine, and in fact describes some of the effects of wine in beneficial terms.

As we take a brief look at wine's benefits described in the Bible, ask yourself, "Am I enjoying life and God?" Life today still brings, at times, nasty and brutish realities, stress, and disappointments. We all need community and friendship to create moments that take us beyond some of the hard realities. If any community should be a custodian of joy and celebration, it is the church as a spiritual community—or the community of our synagogue, or place of spiritual kinship—not an institution.

Psalm 104:14-15, as do other texts, categorizes wine, along with oil, and bread as food. In this same text there is another remarkable insight about wine.

"Gladdening of the heart" is a moderate and beneficial effect of wine. That wine gladdens the heart is a positive benefit of wine. This is the "effect" of wine and is as much a part of the appeal and enjoyment of wine, as taste, or any other characteristic of wine. The "effect" of gladdening the heart or elevating the spirit is not drunkenness. The gladdening of the heart is one of the intrinsic properties of wine!

For some, this is novel—a bit of a stretch, and in fact, could be interpreted as an endorsement for drunkenness, but it is not. The biblical texts are clear in condemning drunkenness (Proverbs 20:1), but texts like Psalm 104:15 speak of a gladdening of the heart, which may be likened to a lifting or lightening of our spirit that produces a sense of well being.

Other verses describe "gladdening of the heart" as a positive effect or characteristic of wine. Ecclesiastes 9:7 says, "Go eat your food with gladness, and drink your wine with a joyful heart." Ecclesiates10:19 proclaims, "A feast is made for laughter, and wine makes life merry." Zechariah 9:15 says, "They will drink and roar as with wine." Further, Zechariah 10:7 says, "... and their hearts will be glad as with wine. Their children will see it and be joyful; their hearts will rejoice in the Lord." Judges 9:13 speaks of wine that cheers both God and men. 2 Samuel 13:28 describes Amnon in high spirits from drinking wine.

The point is simply that "gladdening of the heart" is a positive benefit of drinking wine. Gladdening of the heart is a state of elevated spirit, a sense of lightheartedness, merriment, and a sense of wellbeing. It is good when people come together in a lighter spirit and enjoy the company of one another, and break bread together. Is God not pleased when this happens?

The words of Proverbs 31:6-7 are medicinal:

> Give beer to those who are perishing, wine to those who
> are in anguish; let them drink and forget their poverty
> and remember their misery no more.

Does this mean "drown your sorrows" with drink? Is this really what God is saying? Is this not a form of escapism, denial, and "substance abuse" that helps us deny our reality rather than face it?

In biblical culture, wine is known to have a beneficial effect for a person experiencing emotional distress, and is prescribed as a treatment for gladdening the heart! I think this is the point in providing wine or beer to the perishing. To the person who is dying, drink is prescribed to ease them. To those in anguish or mourning due to death of a loved one, or some deep loss, wine helps to ease the burden. In Jewish tradition, at a funeral, the bereaved was offered ten cups of wine—called the "Cup of Consolation." It is not to help a person deny or escape reality, but to bear up under the burden, the sadness of the time. Doctors prescribe drugs to ease circumstantial anxiety, stress, and depression. In the past and as seen in the Bible, wine performed the same function.

In life, we all face and must bear up under pressures and seasons of sadness and anxieties. Enjoying wine to gladden our hearts is a simple little thing, but a profound blessing and gift from God. It is an appropriate use of wine, not the abuse of wine.

The Bible gives reminders that wine is a gift from God with many benefits. Many of the positive benefits of wine can be reversed when we abuse wine by drinking too much and becoming drunk. (See Chapter 9 on the health benefits of wine.) The positive benefit of wine to our spirit comes through moderation. Many of the "gladdening of the heart" benefits are reversed when we abuse the gift. Drunkenness causes destructive behaviors in some instances, and can cause negative consequences such as depression—just like too much food, and the wrong foods, cause obesity, and a multitude of negative health conditions.

Another interesting Old Testament event describes another benefit of wine:

> When David had gone a short distance beyond the summit, there was Ziba, the steward of Mephibosheth, waiting to meet him. He had a string of donkeys saddled and loaded with two hundred loaves of bread, a hundred cakes of raisins, a hundred cakes of figs and a skin of wine. The king asked Ziba, "Why have you brought these?" Ziba answered, "The donkeys are for the king's household to ride on, the bread and fruit are for the men to eat, and the wine is to refresh those who become exhausted in the desert." (2 Samuel 16:1-2)

Wine has the capacity to restore energy and to animate the exhausted. The wine Ziba provided was an "energy" drink so to speak, to reenergize those who might become weakened or exhausted by the heat of the desert. This is the meaning in Zechariah 9:15—"they will drink and roar as with wine"— the energizing, animating, restorative quality of wine. It was used in battle to restore a soldier's energy, and to refresh him for battle.

Deuteronomy 7:13 is a declaration of God to bless the community. Wine is in the list of blessings. The words bless, blessed, and blessing appear all through the Scriptures. The meaning of these words is simple. To bless is to confer prosperity upon or enrich! "Bless" sums up in one word all the good that God desires to bring to everyone. To drink a glass of wine is to drink abundance, prosperity, and enrichment—all in a glass!

Wine possesses a restorative, refreshing capacity to give us energy when depleted, but the foremost quality of wine is gladness of heart.

"To Spirit" is our first toast!

CHAPTER 9

A TOAST TO HEALTH!

What A Glass Of Wine Can Do
For Your Body

*Stop drinking only water, and use a little wine because of
your stomach and your frequent illnesses. (I Timothy 5:23)*

The Apostle Paul tells his friend to use a little wine for
his health. Back then the medicinal value of wine was known
and prescribed. Paul's associate Timothy was known to be a bit
frail and frequently ill. Paul's solution: drink a little wine!

Further examination of the Bible from the earlier days
of the Old Testament, also, testifies to the health and medicinal
values attributed to wine.

We have a book at home as a handy reference: *Foods
That Heal. Foods That Harm.*[28] We often look to this reference
to sharpen the finer points of our diet. The reference frequently
includes wine as a food that heals.

The Bible is also prescriptive in the use of wine. The
first and foremost principle is that of moderation. Moderation
applies to all of life, but we will limit our consideration to
what we take into our bodies—food and drink. Gluttony is the
opposite of moderation when it comes to food. Gluttony, or
just plain overeating, leads to obesity. Obesity leads to all kinds
of diseases leading to a poor quality of life, and it certainly can
shorten lives. Eating disorders abound in our American society
today, and obesity is epidemic.

Growing up in the South, I constantly heard sermons about drinking, and regardless of the subject of a sermon, included parenthetical insertions against drinking. I can say in all honesty, however, that I never heard a sermon on gluttony. The simple practice of moderation would do so much for a healthier, happier, more vibrant life.

Health Benefits Of Wine From Recent Studies And Research

So, what can a glass of wine do for our bodies? What is the prescription? What is moderation from a health benefit perspective? Examining the wisdom of the Bible, in light of advances in modern medical science, we can find the answers.

Moderation is a constant theme in all studies and discoveries about the health benefits of wine. Moderate consumption of wine produces the maximum health benefit. In general, two four-ounce glasses of red wine a day for men, and one four-ounce glass per day for women is the general recommendation. Researchers go on to say that more or less than that amount reduces the heath benefit—some studies say it actually negates the health benefit.

If you enjoy wine, there may be occasions when you exceed the recommended intake. And it is usually, just that, an occasion marking something special in life: a wedding, an anniversary, a milestone, or just having a good time with family and friends. These are times we may have a little more wine than usual because it is a festive moment, a celebration, and the wine is good, and the camaraderie special. These are exceptional occassions; but as the normal daily intake of wine goes, moderation gives the maximum heath benefit.

You do not have to justify drinking wine on the basis "for medicinal purposes" only. You are invited to enjoy it in the presence of God, to celebrate and mark occasions, to appreciate God's goodness, provision, and blessing, and to enhance gatherings with friends and family. The biblical text holds up wine as a gift and blessing from God. Even if wine did not have health and medicinal qualities, it remains a gift and a blessing, but since wine does possess these added benefits, wine is all the more a gift.

New findings of the health-giving properties of wine are announced almost weekly. While many studies affirm the moderate use of any alcohol including beer or spirits, wine continues to be singled out from other alcoholic beverages as the superior beverage for health. No other food or beverage decreases the overall mortality or the incidence of heart attacks than red wine. One study recommends one or two four-ounce glasses of red wine a day for men to decreases the risk of heart attack by 30 to 50 percent. The study suggests that men with hypertension have a 30 percent lower risk of a heart attack if they drink a glass or two of wine a day. This finding comes from scientists at the Harvard School of Public Health and published in *Annals of Internal Medicine*.[29]

Scientists have identified over 1000 ingredients in red wine—flavonoids and phenol compounds—that work as a team to protect the heart. Flavonoids in red wine decrease clotting tendencies of blood, reducing the incidence of stroke.

Resveratrol is the most significant compound found in red wine and other plants, and is the focus of much research today. Compared to white wines, red wines contain 50 to 100 times more resveratrol, which is found in grape skins. Resveratrol helps prevent fungus from growing on the grape skin. In humans, resveratrol increases HDL (good cholesterol) which carries away LDL (bad cholesterol) from artery walls reducing the amount of plaque that builds up in the arteries.

Headlines such as "CAN WE SLOW AGING?" and "LIVE FOREVER?" herald much of the latest research on aging. However, the question of aging and living forever are not only scientific questions, but are spiritual questions as well. It is quite the subject to contemplate. While I can't imagine, and do not believe in the finality of death, I can't imagine the idea of living forever. However, the Bible says, that God has put eternity in the heart of every human being, and the words of

Jesus echo the same truth. In the truest sense of being, we are all going to live forever. It's a mystery, but a reality.

Again, here is what scientists are tracking. At MIT, a study led by Dr. Leonard Guarente and Dr. David Sinclair fed three groups of middle-aged mice three different diets. One group was fed what is considered to be the normal diet of mice. They showed no unusual traits or behaviors, and no change in their life-span. The second group of mice were fed a high-calorie, high-fat diet. These mice gained weight and developed fatty livers, heart trouble, other problems, and died earlier. The third group got the high-calorie, high-fat diet, and resveratrol—the compound found in wine. These mice got fat, but were as healthy as lean mice.[30]

Scientists are now engaged in studies of resveratrol's effect on humans. The MIT study and numerous other studies are finding evidence that resveratrol may also protect against aging-related diseases.

The bottom line is that resveratrol essentially boosts the body's metabolic rate, which may mimic the slow-aging effects of a calorie-restricted diet—seemingly slowing the aging process. Scientists have discovered that when animals live on 30 to 40 percent fewer calories, they become resistant to most age-related diseases—cancer, heart disease, diabetes, and Alzheimer's—and they live 30 to 50 percent longer! If you enjoy wine, you might as well bet on the potential health and aging benefit of red wine by having your daily intake. A question around our household these days is, "Have you had your red wine today?" What a delightful discipline! If white wines are your favorite, take heart, more and more research suggests that the health benefits of red and white may be equal. Additional studies related to the benefits of resveratrol in red (and white) wine continue to be conducted.

Another study suggests that drinking Cabernet Sauvignon specifically (That's right, the mice in this study drank Cabernet Sauvignon!) may help sharpen the mind and reduce Alzheimer's disease. "We have demonstrated what prior epidemiological studies have found: There is a beneficial relationship between red wine and the mind," says lead author Giulo Maria Pasinetti, a neuroscience professor at Mount Sinai School of Medicine in New York. This study appears in the journal Federation of American Societies for Experimental Biology. Resveratrol reduced levels of a protein called amyloid-beta peptides. These proteins clump, killing surrounding brain cells, which causes short-term memory loss, reducing judgment and attention span. The study affirmed that it was the polyphenols in the red wine, not the alcohol, that does the work.

Another study indicates that the Mediterranean diet including red wine may deter Alzheimer's disease. The study also upheld the practice of moderation demonstrating that a glass or two of wine with the Mediterranean diet meal was a positive scoring factor, while drinking no wine or drinking more than two glasses negated wine's contribution to deterring Alzheimer's. This comes from research published in the *Annals of Neurology* by lead author Nikolas Scarmeas, a neurologist at Columbia University.[31]

One study published in the journal *Cell* suggests that resveratrol may boost muscle endurance.

Other studies about the health benefits of wine have shown that another red wine antioxidant killed cancer cells in an experiment indicating that it may present a promising approach to treating leukemia and lymphomas.

Drinking wine may also help halt arthritis. A Swedish study found that low and steady doses of alcohol slowed the onset of rheumatoid arthritis in laboratory mice. The speculation is that, again, the one- or two-glass a day rule would apply.

Light to moderate drinking is not associated with being overweight or obese suggests a study reported by the British Medical Journal. Dutch researchers reporting at the American Heart Association's 47th Annual Conference on Cardiovascular Disease Epidemiology and Prevention, stated:

Our study showed that long-term, light alcohol intake among middle-aged men was associated not only with lower cardiovascular and all-cause death risk, but also with longer life expectancy at age 50.[32]

We are discovering more and more about the health-giving properties of wine consumed in moderation. The following is a collection of headlines from *Wine Spectator*, and a variety of other newspapers, and journals reporting the virtues of wine:

- Moderate drinking decreases risk of heart attack in hypertensive men, study finds
- Light to moderate wine drinkers live longer, study finds
- Red-wine chemical may help fight ravages of age
- Mediterranean diet may deter Alzheimer's
- Moderate drinkers use Medicare less, study finds
- Wine drinkers may keep weight off, eat healthier
- Regular, moderate drinkers are less likely to be obese
- Study links wine to lower risks of stomach cancer
- Women wine drinkers less likely to suffer dementia
- Moderate alcohol consumption may improve memory
- A drink a day helps the kidneys, research suggests
- Champagne protects brain cells from injury, study finds
- Mediterranean diet helps Alzheimer's patients live longer
- Red wine ingredient may boost muscle endurance
- In study, red wine compound extends lifespan of fish
- Wine, the antidote to a grilled steak
- Alcohol linked to higher risk of breast cancer, study finds
- Drinking alcohol may halt arthritus
- Red-wine antioxidant kills cancer cells in experiment
- Drinking cabernet may cut risk of Alzheimer's
- Some wine grapes contain sleep
- Red wine compound may be good for the gums
- Red wine rich in fiber, study finds
- Alcohol may help fight weight gain in women

- Geneticists uncover how red wine compounds may work to fight prostate cancer
- Staying upbeat: study finds wine may benefit women with heart disease
- Research links red wine to healthier lungs
- Study links wine to lower risk of ovarian cancer
- Wine may fight cancer, but how?
- Live forever!

Are you getting what the above research is saying? I just want to be doubly sure that you are hearing it right! "If you want to keep yourself heathly and thinking clearly into old age, eat a diet rich in fish, fresh vegetables and olive oil, and wash it all down with some wine!" Depending on what translation of the Bible you read, you will come across Jesus beginning a teaching with the words, "Verily, Verily," or "Truly, Truly, I say unto you…" This is the equivalent of saying over a loudspeaker "Now hear this: Wine is good for you!"

Losing It In Paris!

Being in Paris often for a project, I was concerned about coming back each time with more of me than when I left home. Imagine my surprise and astonishment at what happened on each of my trips to France.

I had decided to eat the French diet and see what would happen. In terms of culinary delight, there was no sacrifice. The French consume one-third more fat, including saturated fats, than Americans. The French drink wine daily with their meals. They smoke more, and exercise very little, yet the French have one of the lowest heart-attack rates in the world, and a low incidence of stroke. Health professionals attribute this to moderate amounts of red wine daily. So what happened to me on each of my trips to Paris? For each week eating the French diet and having red wine with meals, I would lose five pounds per week.

I am a firm believer in the French paradox, the Mediterranean diet, and red wine as a staple of the daily diet. We all need to discover the rhythms of diet for our own bodies. I have radically reduced my meat and fat consumption, and sugar intake for health, and a multitude of environmental reasons. Wine (primarily red) remains a staple of the diet, and has been so for over thirty years.

I have also learned that red wine also helps digestion by stimulating acid secretion in the stomach without injuring the mucosal lining. Wine helps prevent gastroenteritis (this may have been one of Timothy's illnesses), and helps prevent travelers' diarrhea. In fact, in studies, red wine actually outperformed bismuth salicylate—the active ingredient in Pepto Bismol. Two glasses of wine with a meal may help prevent food poisoning and dysentery.

Over the last 25 years, I can attest to the value of red wine as the traveler's friend. I tried to carry two small bottles of red wine with me, as I was often in harsh environments in my work and travel for a relief and development organization. I try to take a few ounces of red wine each day "for my stomach's sake." This is not always possible with new security limitations related to air travel. I think it is time to market the three ounce bottle of wine "for medicinal purposes" suited for air travel! The new wine bottle size is sure to have a screw cap so it could carry the tag line, "With a twist reduce the risk!"

I have now visited 70 countries, and sometimes I am not in the best environments health-wise. In over 25 years of international travel, I was ill only once! A second time I became ill from contaminated water—from the water supply of a California city reminding me that a little wine with the water is wise advice!

At times I choose not to drink wine, if the Christian culture I am visiting is adamant in requiring the practices of abstinence. I do not wish to create an unnecessary issue. My own experience, without exception, is that these "Christian" cultures of abstinence and prohibition are rooted in the influence of the North American conservative missionary movement—Jesus plus abstinence!

I am not a physician, so I would not give medical advice to anyone. If one has questions about their use of wine, it should be discussed with a doctor. An informative and helpful book is Dr. Don Colbert's *What Would Jesus Eat?*[33] The book is a great guide to diet, and includes a chapter on wine. The book highlights the diet of Jesus' time, which is essentially what we know as the Mediterranean Diet.

It is important to understand the biblical principle of moderation, especially as it relates to what we eat and drink. Scientific findings in wine and health research continue to reinforce a lifestyle of moderation in wine consumption. The deeper we look, wine in moderation is highly beneficial.

So, as the apostle Paul once said to Timothy, "Drink your wine!"

Lift a glass for the second toast: "To health!"

CHAPTER 10

A TOAST TO LIFE!

What A Glass Of Wine Can Do For Your Life

A feast is made for laughter, and wine makes life merry.
(Ecclesiastes 10:19)

Life is community, and wine is the drink of community.
Do you enjoy life? Do you celebrate life? Are you aware
of blessing? Are you aware of life's energy all around you? Do
you take time to connect, really connect, with God, creation in
all its beauty, and family and friends with all the richness and
color that other people bring to our lives?

Jesus said that he came to show us the way to an
abundant life. Abundance means blessing—God conferring
enrichment and prosperity on one. Throughout the Bible,
God's blessing always included a bountiful harvest and new
wine. The provision of wine was a measure of God's favor.

An abundant life is experienced now. You cannot live
in the past or in the future. Abundance is not there. You can
only live now to enjoy your wine. Wine is more than a beverage
to drink. Wine is like abundance, beauty and creation all in a
bottle. Wine is creation concentrated.

Rabbi Harold Kushner, writing in *To Life: A Celebration
Of Jewish Being And Thinking*, describes the meaning of words of
the toast "To Life!"

They suggest first that Judaism is about how to live, not
just what to believe. They convey an optimistic attitude

toward life, investing our energy in living rather than in worrying about dying, asking us to enjoy the pleasures of this life rather than noticing all the things that are wrong with it, emphasizing life in this world rather than pinning our hopes on finding satisfaction in some world to come.[34]

Kushner continues,

To life conveys a sense of exuberance, a readiness to enjoy the pleasures of this world. It removes from wine, and from other pleasures, the taint of sin and self-indulgence, and invites us to look at all that God has created and find it good.[35]

Uncorking a bottle of wine with others is one of the best antidotes for unconscious living. Wine helps us to create parenthetical moments, time outs, to connect to one another and experience an "all is well" moment.

Around the world, there is a growing consciousness, a resurgence of authentic spirituality, Christians included. They are being released from the chains of a rigid, fearful "have I got it all right?" spirituality that keeps them in the bondage of judgmentalism and self-condemnation. The emerging spirituality is characterized not by what it is against nor what it fears, but by what is embraced, valued, and celebrated. It is an experience of truth that sets you free.

Those experiencing a renewal of spirit are finding a place for passion, enjoyment of life, and a freedom to appreciate the gift of wine. They are discovering these things aren't such odd companions with God and spirituality, but actually go together. Wine points us to the Creator and creation—the same place our spirituality is anchored. Out of earth, water, and sun, the vine and the wine it produces illuminate our spirit bringing us ever closer to the heart of God.

Who, along life's journey, does not desire enrichment and moments of happiness and enjoyment with others? "One another" is so much a part of the spiritual journey, and it is important to discover that life is richer and fuller in relationships with one another.

Have you had the experience of drinking wine with friends, and the wine tastes so good to you, that you plan to buy a bottle of the same wine for another time? You drink the wine another time in another setting, and it doesn't taste quite as good as you remember. It wasn't bad; it just didn't live up to the memory. The occasion that you first enjoyed the wine was a special time, with special people, and at a special place. All the ingredients creating a special moment in life came together. Occasion made the wine taste better! Wine enjoyed in the company of others enhances the taste of wine!

Celebration, community, and just plain fun have to be intentional, otherwise these things tend to not happen. We have to be intentional to celebrate, to commemorate, and to enjoy moments in life with one another. In the Gospel of John, Jesus, after he had given what amounted to a pep talk to his disciples, tells his followers that life can have some pressures, can bring some disappointments, seeming setbacks, and troubles. Yet Jesus tells them they should "…be of good cheer, I have overcome the world." Jesus tells us that those things that beat you down, and weigh you down, he has overcome. That means "we" have overcome! That is worth celebrating!

In the book *Irresistible Revolution*, Shane Claiborne, a self-described "ordinary radical," says,

> *I began to understand what it meant when the curtain of the temple was torn open as Jesus died on the cross. Not only was God redeeming that which was profane, but God was setting all that was sacred free. Now God dwelled not behind the veil in the temple but in the eyes of the dying and the poor, in the ordinary and the mundane, in things like bread and wine, or chai and*

samosas. And whenever two or three of us come together
in community, God is there among us.[36]

The Scriptures are filled with admonitions to enjoy life. For example: "A feast is made for laughter, and wine makes life merry…" (Ecclesiastes 10:19) and "the Lord Almighty will prepare a feast of rich food for all peoples, a banquet of aged wine—the best of meats and the finest of wines" (Isaiah 25:6). Or this: "They will come and shout for joy on the heights of Zion: they will rejoice in the bounty of the Lord—the grain, the new wine…" (Jeremiah 31:12).

Most of my travel over the past twenty-five years was for helping churches around the world. My contribution was through leadership coaching and training in the area of leadership development, building teams, clarifying vision and mission, developing strategy, and spiritual guidance. Many of the leaders and churches I served ministered in difficult and challenging circumstances. The circumstances of their realities would be enough for many, including myself, to want to give up and forget it.

I was regularly challenged by their commitment, perseverance, and determination to prevail. They were committed to transforming their community to make life better for everyone. In spite of the challenging situations they faced, their capacity for love, joy, happiness, and celebration was genuine and infectious. They made a choice to live that way! It is a reminder that our thought is our life—as one thinks, so is he."

It is in these circumstances that I experienced authentic community, and made many friends. We celebrated the goodness of God and life together many times. This is where I learned much about spirituality, commitment, and much about happiness. We drank wine together to the glory of God, and we celebrated the abundance of life in circumstances where it didn't make sense.

My life has been international, and that has deeply impacted and shaped my life and my faith. Traveling the globe, experiencing other cultures, and experiencing faith through the lenses of differing histories and situations have all helped increase my awarness of the cultural dimensions of my spirituality and my faith journey.

Our lives can be rich and that richness comes from our outlook on life. It's as Kushner says about the toast, "To life! Be optimistic and live! Enjoy the pleasures of this life." Find the good in everything, every human being, every gift of God. What does all of this have to do with wine? It is simply that wine "cheers both God and men." Wine transforms the ordinary to the extraordinary. Wine animates conversation. Wine is a magical catalyst to friendships and relationships. The variety of wines invites us to enjoy God's goodness with endless choices of flavors, aromas, and taste. Good wine plus friendship is one of the greatest pleasures of life.

Arriving on the Mediterranean Coast of Spain was always exhilarating. I shared life for many years with the people of the Communidad Cristiana Parque Victoria in Rincon de la Victoria, a suburb of Malaga on the Mediterranean coast of Spain. We worked together for an era of their history. During those days it was common practice to gather in a home or a restaurant and enjoy a meal together—always with good Spanish wine, laughter, and stimulating conversations. I learned from them that we can celebrate in all circumstances, and create moments of fun, enjoyment of people, and enjoyment of good food and wine. They taught me to live in the present moment—to be there with one another.

Spanish red wine was the wine of choice, of course. We were in Spain—a land of wine. I was introduced to the practice of drinking red wine mixed with La Casera (similar to Seven-Up). Being a "purist," I first raised my eyebrow at diluted cold red wine, but discovered it to be a refreshing drink on a hot Mediterranean afternoon. Wine with my Spanish friends was always a special occasion, because of their friendship and acceptance of a "yank."

Grapes aren't grown in the Bahamas, but New Providence Community Church in Nassau, was the first church to ask me to lead a wine tasting at the church. The church is a an international community in outlook, and a gathering place for local artists—and painters, sculptors, and musicians. Nassau has been the site for an informal gathering for theological conversation among a group of friends for over ten years. We have our evening meals together for our lighter moments to relax with one another around food and wine.

In California, I have friends at the Mount Carmel Community Church in Glennville in the foothills of the Sierras. This small church community is the catalyst that brings their larger community together—500 people scattered in a 500 square mile area of Kern County, the largest county in California by land area.

The parties and celebrations this church puts on are very popular with the local, yet widespread, community. People living in Glenville and the surrounding ranches of Kern and Tulare counties could not imagine Christmas without the annual Christmas Dessert at the church. It is ironic that many people move to this area to get away from people, but the infectious community of the church connects with them. Valentine's Day, July 4th, rodeos, and nights on the hillside under a full moon give pause for fun, and merriment complimented by California wine.

Evenings in a home or a backyard with the people of Mount Carmel are accented by some of the most colorful people I have ever met. The community is extraordinarily musically talented. The stories they tell paint a romantic, boisterous portrait of life in this part of creation.

I've participated with the community for more than 25 years, and authentic community has continued unbroken for all those years. It is not a clique. A clique is a closed-off group—there are the insiders and the outsiders—that is not true community. Community is open, dynamic; there are no outsiders. No one is a stranger. That's Mount Carmel

Community Church in Glennville. You're always welcome. There's always room at the table—always plenty of food and wine, and friendship.

In my home back in Texas hill country, I'm part of a growing community of spiritual seekers. These are people on a conscious spiritual journey, who seek to know God and Truth. They all long for safe places to be with others, where no one wears a mask, and all can be themselves without fear of rejection. After all, who we are is all we have. If we are rejected, where else is there to go? Jesus' idea of the Kingdom of God is that we all belong. There are no outsiders possible in the Kingdom as Jesus offers it to us.

I look forward to nights on the patio with family and friends to celebrate life and relax with one another. Food and a glass of wine in the Texas moonlight create a setting second to none.

My wife and I are close friends with another couple. We are good friends going back many years. We are always ready to accept an invitation from Steve and Sarah when they invite us to dinner. Dinner parties in their home are always a great experience. Delicious food and wine are served with genuine hospitality, and the unspoken "we're so glad you're here." Sarah is the master of hospitality and entertaining. Together, Steve and Sarah prepare an altar with a tablecloth for their guests.

Conversation at the table over a meal, where there is no pretense, no required formality to protect our true identity, where we are truly invited to be ourselves, is priceless. If you are not experiencing this now, or if you have never enjoyed the experience, then you need to find it. Create occasion! Invite friends, and get on with it. Don't live lonely. Don't die lonely. Be in community! Drink your wine with others!

What I am describing may appear limited to middle and upper class people. It is true that, for many, wine is an unknown luxury, and beyond their means, but, on so many occasions, I have been invited to a celebration and feast in impoverished settings. Often, we knew the wine being served represented a great sacrifice, and at the same time we knew it was shared in genuine love and hospitality. On more than one occasion, I knew we were being offered the last of food, and the last bottle of wine, but to refuse would not be understood or accepted by our host. Poverty is not a barrier to feasting, celebrating, and welcoming people into your home and community. In contrast, I once met a man at a wine tasting who told me of his wine cellar of some 7000 bottles. He boasted of his plan to drink all 7000 bottles himself finishing the last bottle on his last day of life.

I witness more true poverty among middle and upper classes that are distracted by so many things and options— options that hinder enriching relationships and the enjoyment of life. This impoverishes our spirit. Often, people of lesser means, know the meaning of celebrating and being together with family and friends. It is of such a high value that sacrifice is made to ensure that this is not eliminated from their life. Some of those gatherings are my most memorable.

It is like Shane Claiborne says, "…God dwelled…in things like bread and wine, or chai and samosas. And whenever two or three of us come together in community, God is there among us."

I remember one hot afternoon in Northern Nigeria being invited into a temporary grass hut of a nomadic Fulani herdsman. We were offered cookies and warn Coca-Cola with warmer hospitality. God was present in community in grass huts with dirt floors in Northern Africa as we broke biscuits and shared warm Coca-Cola together. Coca-Cola was the wine of the occasion. There was sacrifice to provide the Coke and biscuits.

I've asked myself what made all of these gatherings so special? What made these occasions similar and extraordinary? What does a lunch in Spain, a meal with friends, coke and biscuits in a grass hut, to a hillside in Glennville, to dinner at my friends' house share in common? I think the answer is in the idea of creating an altar with a tablecloth[37] that includes a few simple elements:

Place. Place is created with a few simple nuances that say, "we are glad you are here." This can be as simple as place cards identifying seating at the table; a little decoration, a flower arrangement, or a candle. Place is created, not just space provided.

Friendship. We get together in friendship and together enjoy God's goodness and provision, including the food and wine we take together at this meal.

Thankfulness. Thankfulness and appreciation can be expressed in simple prayer or a toast to God for friends, life, and blessing. This is the wine-stained altar to which we come.

Laughter. Laughter is a medicine. We must laugh! The absence of laughter is a serious disorder, and it must be treated. We must learn to lighten up! Laughter should be inevitable when the ingredients of the altar with a tablecloth are put before us.

Wine. Wine that "gladdens the heart" that "cheers both God and man," because "a feast is made for laughter, and wine makes life merry. Drink your wine with a joyful heart." A toast can be offered for the wine. We can learn from Jewish tradition and practice, as there is no communal, religious, or family life without wine. Each Sabbath begins and ends with a cup of wine, and a prayer such as, "Blessed are you O Lord Our God …for creating the fruit of the vine." A prayer of this nature is always offered. Of course, the mere appreciation and thanksgiving for the wine can go unspoken…but understood.

Authenticity. Authenticity cannot be created; it is an expression of character. But you must be authentic to experience community at the altar with a tablecloth.

Because of the speed at which we live and the fragmentation caused by all the little things we must do in order to sustain our lifestyles, little to nothing is left for living in the present, much less experiencing an awareness of God and one another. Make time for rest, people, pleasure, and restoration of your spirit. Take the time to see, smell, and savor the wine.

Relationship is the wine of a vibrant, happy, and meaningful life. Wine is the drink of relationship—a restoring, refreshing, and reviving tonic.

With three toasts, we share together what a glass of wine can do for us. In "To Health!" we nourish our bodies. With "To Spirit!" we discover what a glass of wine can do to elevate our emotional and spiritual wellbeing. "To Life!" challenges us to live with happiness, exuberance, and friendship enjoying the pleasures God has set before us.

CHAPTER 11

ENJOYING WINE IN THE HERE AND NOW

My cup runneth over! (Psalm 23)

The Bible is a rich treasure of information about wine. The Bible story about wine sets forth that wine is a gift from God to be enjoyed. The Bible gives an ancient record of wine dating further back than any other source. It provides a remarkable "wine appreciation course." The Bible is not typically thought of as a wine guide, but it provides us with insight about wine and wine drinking. The grape vine is the most mentioned plant in the Bible. Wine, the vine, and the vineyard are used in the Old Testament with powerful imagery, analogy, and metaphor to teach and express great spiritual truth. In the New Testament, Jesus uses the vine, wine, and the vineyard as teaching tools to illustrate the way of life he is introducing.

The Bible—Old and New Testament—is the life source for guidance and direction for Christians, and the Old Testament for Jews. Those on other spiritual paths also seek spiritual guidance from the Scriptures. And in the context of the biblical narrative, wine is included in the information, insight, and instruction given on a multiplicity of subjects.

Here is a summary of some of the facts, insights, and knowledge the Bible sheds on wine:

- Wine is a gift from God to be enjoyed.
- Noah is the first known farmer to grow grapes and make wine.
- Wine cheers both God and man.

- Wine is categorized as food.
- Many varieties and styles of wines were known in biblical times.
- Wine is a sign of blessing.
- Wine is so valued that lack of wine was demoralizing to the society.
- Wine gladdens the heart.
- Wine can elevate the spirit of the bereaved.
- Wine has medicinal qualities.
- Wine is to be consumed in moderation.
- Jesus drank wine.
- Wine, vine, and vineyard were so commonly known that they made excellent object lessons for teaching.

A Brief Guide To Enjoying Wine In The Here And Now

The following brief guide will introduce some of the basics of wine tasting and drinking. For some, this is a basic review, and for others the guide is a starting point. Remember, wine should be approachable, not complicated, but simple and enjoyable. Ultimately, you are your own best wine guide.

What Is A Good Wine?

Most often this is the first question I'm asked about wine, "What is a good wine?" And the answer is always the same, and delightfully simple: A good wine is a wine that you like! That's why no one can tell you what a good wine is for you. Only you know your palate. Admittedly, there are some wine snobs who will tell you what is good and what is not for everyone.

While you know your palate best, many excellent wine educators, writers, and tasters can enhance your knowledge, understanding, and appreciation of wine. A few of my favorites are Andrea Robinson,[38] Master Sommelier and wine author; Kevin Zraley,[39] renowned wine educator; and Robert Parker,[40] who must have the best palate in the world. These three are unpretentious, approachable, knowledgeable, well respected, and reliable. I enjoy their tasting notes and wine recommendations, and find they are consistently reliable. But remember, no palate is the same. You might find wines at times that have a high recommendation and rating, and may even be on the expensive end, but you taste the wine and you don't like it. It happens. And don't feel bad if the next wine you drink is a $10 red and you like it! That happens too!

Let's look at some wine basics that help us get the most out of our wine experience.

Tasting Wine

Wine becomes an experience, when we take the time to consciously appreciate wine. The experience is enhanced when we taste wines with family and friends, because we talk about the wine when we are with others who are sharing the experience with us.

We live fast, drink fast, and eat fast. Wine is the nectar of slowness, and to take the time to experience our wine is a great way to relax. Because of our fast-pace of life, I have adopted the five-step-wine-tasting-process, but wine writers use different acronyms to guide the tasting process. Some outline three steps, others more.

By making wine tasting a five-step experience, we make a little extra time to concentrate on the wine experience. These five easy steps—beginning with the letter "S"—will help you get the most out of wine tasting since wine stimulates all our senses! Pour a little wine into your glass—an ounce or so, and begin.

SEE the color of the wine. Wine possesses an array of beautiful colors. Take time to examine the color of the wine. Tilt your glass away from you and look at the wine against a well-lit white background, and consciously take in the color. Describe the color. Does it sparkle? Shimmer? Is it brilliant? Depending on style, red wines can range from dark pink to dark purple. Red wine gains color from contact with the grape skins. White wines will range from pale straw to golden. God created in color, so see the color in the wine!

SWIRL the wine in your glass. Swirling releases the vapors of the wine, releasing the scents to your nose. The scents open you to the flavors of the wine. The flavors are detected from the scents, and taste is identified by the tongue. Don't fill your glass so full that you can't swirl the wine. The swirl is an important step to smelling and tasting the wine.

SMELL the wine after swirling it around three or four times, and don't be afraid to stick your nose right in the glass to capture as much as you can of the wine's scents, flavors, and aromas. How many different smells can you identify? Over time you will be able to identify more smells. Smell is the queen of our senses distinguishing a complexity of aromas and flavors.

SIP and taste the wine, but take a mouthful and swish it around for awhile. A mouthful assures that you will get the taste of the wine. To review, swirling helps you get a better smell of the wine, and that gives you a fuller taste.

SAVOR the wine in your mouth. Move it around so that the wine comes into contact with all the taste receptors of your tongue—all 10,000 or so! Science is discovering more and more about the tongue. It was long thought that humans had only four taste receptors—salty, sweet, sour, and bitter. Scientists are discovering that the tongue is more complex. Now we learn there is a fifth receptor called umami. Umami is described as a savory, brothy taste, but umami interacts with the other receptors for a complexity in taste. Scientists are not certain how umami works together with the other receptors, but it does. Umami could help explain the complexities of the taste of wine, and reinforces the practice of taking time to savor wine to appreciate all the tastes presented by a wine.

By taking time to savor the wine, you will taste the subtleties and nuances. Another thing you can identify with the sip and savor is the body of the wine. Body means weight. Sommelier Andrea Robinson uses milk to explain body. She says, think of skim milk which is light and thin; whole milk has a greater viscosity; and half-and-half coats your palate. The body of wine has nothing to do with the quality of wine. Body is another sensation you can experience that tells you about the character of the wine.

When should you go through the five-step tasting process? Any time you're tasting wine! It's true—you won't do this every time you have a bottle of wine with your meal in a restaurant. Onlookers might think you're anal, a little crazy, or worse, a wine snob. Actually, you will create a habit of consciously tasting your wine in restaurants, or anywhere you have wine. Before long you will catch yourself swirling all beverages—even milk! But when you have your own wine tastings with friends at home, take the time to go through the deliberate process of tasting the wine. After tasting, try to describe what you've tasted to others. It's a good exercise to translate taste into words.

Of course, when you are tasting wine in a winery tasting room, or a wine-tasting event, go all out to taste. That is why you and everyone else are there. In these environments, you can add a few more steps—slurp, gurgle, and spit! While this might not sound proper, at a wine tasting it is absolutely acceptable. I find most people don't like to spit out wine they taste, but if you are going to taste many wines, spitting will serve you well. After you've swallowed five or six wines, your senses will be dulled and you will miss out on the many nuances and subtleties of the wine.

The Classic Wine Grape Varieties

The Bible speaks of "wines of all kinds." A variety of wines were known in biblical times, and many wines were likely known during the first and second temple periods in Israel. By the time of Jesus, the Greeks were the leading wine producers, widely exporting to the known world, but Rome was emerging as the leading producer and exporter.

Karen MacNeil in *The Wine Bible* says that there are 24,000 names for varieties of grapes representing about 5,000 different varieties. Of those 5,000, only 150 are planted in commercially significant amounts, and only six to nine grapes are considered classic varieties.[41] I don't know of anyone who has tasted the 5000 varieties, let alone all 24,000! The 150, yes—and the classics most certainly. One of the fun things about wine, is the chase—to discover and experience new and different wines. We will never run out of new wines to try. To attempt tasting all 24,000 varieties in one year would require a person to taste 65 wines each day!

The classic varieties are a great place to begin developing your knowledge about wine. What makes a wine grape a classic? A classic variety is one that has shown high quality over a long period of time and is produced in many places with high quality.

If you have not tasted all of the classics, you have your first goal or threshold to achieve in wine enjoyment. This is the only assignment from this book: Taste the classics!

I've focused on six classics—three reds and three whites. I've also featured a few more important and popular varieties.

I'm sure many of you are further down the road in your wine knowledge, but if you are a wine novice, by tasting the top six classics, you are well on your way to becoming more familiar with different styles of wine—more importantly, introducing your palate to distinctively different wines.

All six varieties can be found in your grocery store wine aisle, and at wine shops. To enhance your tasting of the classics, taste all six in one sitting. By tasting all at once, you will experience the diversity of tastes and textures offered by different wines, and that's just the beginning to the wonderful world of wine.

Taste the wines in this order to fully appreciate their characteristics: Whites first: Riesling, Sauvignon Blanc, and then Chardonnay. Then taste the reds: Pinot Noir, Merlot, and finally Cabernet Sauvignon. The order takes you from the sweeter, lighter wines to the dryer, more complex wines. Having a group of people to participate in the tasting makes it a more fun and enjoyable experience.

A word on the cost of a wine—you can drink good wine at $10 a bottle! More and more people are cost-conscious, and don't want to spend $25 or $50 for a bottle of wine. Price is not a guarantee of quality. Finding good quality wine at the $10 price point is an achievable challenge. More and more good wines are available under $10. When you want to splurge, the $10 to $20 category will richly reward you. You can choose to spend more for a bottle of wine, or Champagne, or other sparkling wines for special occasions. Having a good wine merchant to guide you in these purchases is helpful. When you describe what you are looking for to a knowledgeable wine merchant, you are going to get a good recommendation. Don't be disappointed, however, when you buy a wine you don't particularly like—that's part of the chase. Go on to try other wines!

And final words on taste—don't be overwhelmed by multiple-word descriptions of the aroma and flavor of wine. Some tasters who describe wines are "hyper-tasters"—having an exceptional sense of smell and taste. Their heightened sense shouldn't deter you if your best description is, "I like this wine." If you can identify at least two or three scents, flavors, or aromas of a wine, you're doing well. I learn from the hyper-tasters, and try to identify the many characteristics they identify, and keep in mind that no palate is the same.

The Classic Whites
These are the three classic white grapes:

Riesling
Riesling may be the most unappreciated and underrated wine in the USA. Riesling is mostly a light-bodied wine, fruity, and crisp. Many Rieslings are sweet wines, but there are plenty of medium-sweet (off-dry)—as well as dry (not sweet) wines. Rieslings can be fragrant and floral, like a meadow in your mouth—and acidity gives it that crisp sensation in your mouth. Germany and Alsace, France produce some of

the world's best Riesling. Also, try Rieslings from Washington State, California, Oregon, New York, and Australia. I enjoy Riesling on the patio on a hot Texas afternoon. A German Riesling was the first white wine I ever tasted, and remains a personal favorite.

Sauvignon Blanc

Sauvignon Blanc possesses a distinctive character with lively aromas of grapefruit, grass, herbs, and citrus. Most Sauvignon Blanc is medium-bodied. Compare it to the full-bodied texture of the Chardonnay, to experience the difference of the mouth feel of a full-bodied to the mouth feel of a medium-bodied wine. Enjoy Sauvignon Blanc from New Zealand, California, Washington State, and France's Loire Valley, and Bordeaux. There are many great Sauvignon Blanc values around ten dollars.

Chardonnay

Widely produced in many styles—all over the world, Chardonnay is the top selling white wine in the USA. Winemakers like Chardonnay because it is very adaptable to climate, and can be made in different styles beginning with whether the wine will be oaked (put in oak barrels) for a period of time for aging, or unoaked. Unoaked Chardonnay can be steely, (or minerally) such as those from Chablis in France's Burgundy region, to the fruity aromas of pineapple, apple, and tropical fruits. Most Chardonnay is oaked, however, tasting of toast, smoke, spice, butter, vanilla, or butterscotch. Chardonnay wines are full bodied—a rich white wine. Look to California for an excellent range of Chardonnay in many styles.

The Classic Reds

These are the three classic red grapes:

Pinot Noir

The first word that comes to my mind for Pinot Noir is sensual—because most Pinot Noirs are silky smooth in your mouth. Pinot Noir is a light-bodied wine, lighter in color, and less tannic than Cabernet Sauvignon. Well-made Pinots exhibit aromas and flavors of cherries, baked-cherries, mushrooms, earth, cedar, cigar, plums and chocolates. Two regions of the world merit special recognition for Pinot Noir: Burgundy in France, and Oregon. Pinot Noir is the grape of red Burgundy wines. Burgundy is made up of so many smaller vineyards and producers, that it's challenging to sort out. But, for a Pinot Noir experience, try a red Burgundy. Burgundy wines are expensive, but some lower-priced ones are available. Oregon is known for Pinot Noir producing some great wines, and an abundance of very good Pinots. Also, try Pinots from California and New Zealand.

Merlot

I've noticed when a specific wine is mentioned in a movie or television script, it is most always Merlot. It is a short name that most people know, and Merlot is likely popular in the USA because it is a softer—less tannic wine. However, Merlot and Cabernet Sauvignon share many of the same characteristics, and can be easily confused when tasting blind. Merlot and Cabernet Sauvignon combined are the top-selling red wines. Both varieties produce excellent wines in all price ranges. Some primary flavors you will taste with Merlot include plums, chocolate, baked-cherries, as well as blackberry and cassis like in Cabernet Sauvignon. Try Merlots from California, Washington State, Chile, and France—from Pomerol and St.-Emilion.

Cabernet Sauvignon

Some of the world's best wines are made from Cabernet Sauvignon grapes. Dark in color, Cabernet produces a more intense, flavorful wine—big and bold. Most are medium- to full-bodied wines. Cabernet Sauvignon tends to be high in tannins, the natural compound that comes from the skins, stems, and pits of the grapes. Tannin also comes from the oak barrels. Tannin is a tactile sensation that creates a dry, smack-your-lips sensation. So, with aged Cabernet Sauvignon, you are going to experience that dry sensation produced by tannin. There are softer styles of Cabernet that are fruity and medium-bodied. Some dominant flavors of Cabernet are blackcurrants or cassis. We don't eat blackcurrants every day, so to help educate your palate, pick up some in the market when they are available. Taste them, and then taste a Cabernet Sauvignon, and see if you can identify the aroma and flavor. Blackberry, mint, eucalyptus, and plum are some other tastes you will frequently detect in a Cab. Cabernet Sauvignon is the grape of the Bordeaux region of France, with the exception of Pomerol and St-Emilion where the grape is Merlot. Try Cabernet Sauvignon from Bordeaux, California, Washington State, and for somewhere different, Texas! In addition, Australia, Chile, Argentina, and South Africa also produce Cabernet Sauvignon.

The six classics are a great starting place, to become familiar with wine—learning the scents, flavors, and tastes of the various varieties. If you are familiar with these wines, you are familiar with most of the wine produced around the world. There will be no end to discovering new wines beyond the classic six. Here are a few other important wines to check out.

Other Notable White Wines

Pinot Grigio/Pinot Gris

These are the same grape—Pinot Grigio is the Italian name and Pinot Gris is used for wines from California, Oregon, and elsewhere. Pinot Grigio is the most imported wine from Italy. Oregon is an important producer of Pinot Gris. The wine is medium- to full-bodied, less acidic, and easy drinking.

Chenin Blanc

Chenin Blanc wines range from sweet to very dry, and everything in between. Don't overlook this medium-bodied wine with flavors of pears, peaches, apples, melons, and apricots—sounds like the fruit cocktail of wine! Try a Vouvray from the Loire Valley in France, along with wines from South Africa, Washington State, and, Texas.

Gewurztraminer

I don't want the pronunciation to deter you from trying this wine, so here is the pronunciation: geh VAIRTZ trah mee ner. Gewurtztraminer is full-bodied with a floral aroma and flavors of apricot, and sometimes honey, and spice. France's Alsace region is where you find the great Gewurtztraminer—dry with flavors that are a party on the palate.

Semillon

Often blended with Sauvignon Blanc, Semillon is low in acid with flavors of lanolin (seriously), and can take on a lush, honey flavor with age. It is an important wine in Australia for white blends, i.e. Semillon-Chardonnay. Australia also produces dry Semillon wines.

Viognier

This grape from France's Rhone Valley is medium- to full-bodied, with low acid, and a floral aroma and a subtle flavor of apricot. If you want a change from Chardonnay, try this wine. It is also produced in southern France and California.

Other Notable Red Wines

Syrah/Shiraz

The Syrah grape really belongs among the classics. Syrah (French) and Shiraz—the name popularized by Australia's labeling of the wine—are the same grape. The home of Syrah is the northern part of France's Rhone Valley, but the Australian wines popularized Shiraz in the United States. Shiraz's flavor, moderate price, and easy to pronounce name, help make this a popular wine. Generally full-bodied and dark purple in color, its flavors include smoke, pepper, and berries. Try French Syrah, which is a big and bold wine. Australian Shiraz styles include medium-bodied, fruity wines. Also, try Shiraz from California.

Zinfandel

Zinfandel, fondly called Zin by its fans is a red grape. White Zinfandel, the most successful commercial wine, is made from the red grape. Zin has been around for a long time in California. Zinfandel makes a jammy, tannic, wine with flavors of blackberry, raspberry, and spice. It ranges from medium- to full-body wines.

Malbec

Argentina leads the way for Malbec today, and it is the Argentina Malbecs that have made the wine popular in the States. Malbec is a blending grape in Bordeaux, but for some reason Argentina has great success with Malbec. Argentineans, on average, eat a half-pound of beef per day, and what do they drink with their beef?—Malbec! Malbecs are smooth, velvety, medium- to full-bodied with notes of blackberry, vanilla and spice, and plum. Malbecs are available across the price ranges with nuances of style and taste.

Sangiovese

Sangiovese is the red grape of Tuscany, but you may know the wine by the name Chianti—one of two principle districts where it is grown—the other is Brunello di Montalcino. Italian wines are labeled by region, so when you drink these wines, you are drinking Sangiovese. Sangiovese is now also grown in California and Washington State. Body varies from light to full depending on the location of the vineyards, and how the wine is made. The wines are fruity with the taste of cherry, tart, and sometimes earthy. Chianti has outgrown the old image of cheap wine in a round straw-covered bottle—you've probably seen them.

Tempranillo

This is Spain's main red grape. Tempranillo is light- to medium-bodied, with aromas and flavors of cherries, and scents of vanilla from oak. Many Tempranillos are aged in oak for two years and some up to five to seven years. Spanish wines are increasing in popularity, driven by price and quality.

After tasting the six classic wines and some of the other recommended varieties, you can continue to try other varieties to expand your wine experience. For those who say, "I like wine, but I don't know much about it," the six classics, and the others noted will give you a foundation for understanding and appreciating wine, because tasting is the final word in wine!

Two additional wine categories deserve a brief introduction: Champagne and sparkling wine, and dessert wine.

To be called Champagne, a wine must come from the Champagne region of France, but you will see some producers use the name anyway. Champagne and sparkling wine are thought by many as only a drink for a special occasion or festive event, and the bubbly is in itself, festive. There is something special about those bubbles! So, enjoy them for those special occasions, but think of Champagne and sparkling wines as food wines. Champagne or sparkling wine make a great match for salmon, for example. These wines don't have to be expensive. A great variety of sparkling wines and Champagnes are economically to moderately priced and, you'll have no difficulty discovering high quality wines in the lower price range. Include these wines in your exploration and tasting, and try them with food. Beyond Champagne, look for excellent sparkling wines from Italy, Spain, California, and Washington to get started.

Dessert wines are unctuous, and they are sweet, but good ones are not cloying, but well balanced. An infinite variety of dessert wines are available today from many different grapes and regions. Dessert wines can be the dessert themselves. When matched with a dessert, the rule is that the wine needs to be as sweet or sweeter than the dessert. If the wine is less sweet than the dessert, it will not taste good. Try the prized Sauternes of France, a German or Canadian ice wine—literally picked frozen on the vine, or a sweet Riesling from Washington. Dessert wines are amazing taste experiences. Don't neglect to try one!

Screw Caps, Corks, And Romance

The screw cap will never replace the cork in my opinion. The romance and ceremony of uncorking a bottle of wine is part of the enjoyment of the wine. Your sommelier by simply turning the screw cap and presenting the bottle of wine at your table will never replace the ceremony of uncorking. The screw top may provide a better seal than a cork for wines, especially those made for immediate consumption, but this is debated. The trend is away from screw caps and the plastic corks. Many in the industry believe the percentage of wines with bad corks is exaggerated, and is probably only one percent. In the meantime don't avoid wines with screw caps. Some wineries are using screw caps for their premium wines. It's not the negative thing it was once perceived to be, but don't worry, the cork is here to stay.

Wine Is The Drink Of Moderation

Wine is by its nature and character the drink of moderation. Wine has lower alcohol content than liquor and spirits. People like to talk about wine with one another, and conversation and community are, in themselves, agents of moderation. The alcohol content of most wines falls between 12% and 13.5%. Some wines can be as low as 8% or even lower such as a German Riesling. Some wines like a California Cabernet Sauvignon might be as high as 15%. In comparison, liquors and spirits are generally in the 40% to 50% level in comparison. This is not to condemn liquor and spirits, but merely to point out that different quantities equal moderation based on alcohol content.

Moderation in all things is a biblical principle that not only applies to wine consumption, but all things. Percentage of alcohol is not really the measure of moderation, but it is just common sense that the measure of moderation will vary by the percent of alcohol and the quantity consumed.

Moderation is a personal matter. Most people know their capacity and abide by their experience. You can determine and know moderation for yourself, and remember the health benefit of wine is based on moderate daily drinking—two glasses for men, one for women.

Wine serves moderation by its lower alcohol content. Wine serves moderation by its social character—throughout history wine has brought people together, and that in itself reinforces moderation.

Wine is unique among beverages, a direct result of agriculture and farming. Many growers tell their story of faith experienced every year during the growing season, and at the harvest. You plant and practice good viticulture, but it takes faith in the end.

Wrapping The Bible Around Wine

The Bible contains narratives of the faith journeys of many who have gone before us including the narrative of Jesus' life and message. The Bible is a story to guide and enlighten us on our spiritual path. Embedded in the biblical narrative, is the Bible's own story of wine, that is essentially a wine-appreciation course—"Wine & Spirit 101."

I created the term oenotheology to communicate the Bible's wealth of knowledge about wine. Oenotheology is the science and scientific study of winemaking, and theology is the study of God's attributes and relations to everything in the universe. God has a relationship to wine. Oenotheology is the study of that relationship. Oenotheology includes the knowledge—the joyfully consistent theme, that wine is a gift from God to be enjoyed!

To those of you who enjoy wine and seek to know God, may your journey continue to new horizons—new wines, new conversations, and new visions of life. May you join the Psalmist and say, "My cup runneth over!"

To all, may your cup overflow with new wine, and the new wine of knowing God.

ENDNOTES

1 Attributed to Johann Wolfgang von Goethe, 1771.

2 Cited in Charles Seltman, *Wine in the Ancient World*, London, Routledge & Kegan Paul, 1957, pp. 131-132.

3 Yaron Goldfisher and Eliezer Sacks, *The Wine Route of Israel*, Tel Aviv, Cordinata Publishing House, 2006, p. 15.

4 Hugh Johnson, *Vintage*, New York, Simon and Schuster, 1989, p. 18.

5 André Dominé, *Wine*, Potsdam, h.f.ullmann, Tanden Verlag GmbH for the English edition, 2008, p. 740.

6 Ibid., p.740.

7 David Alexander and Pat Alexander, editors, *Eerdman's Handbook to the Bible*, Grand Rapids, Michigan, William B. Eerdmans Publishing House, 1973, p. 354.

8 The letter was revealed to me in 1994 by a North American missionary serving in Germany with a large North American mission agency. The letter was written by his supervisor from his office in the United States.

9 Kenneth L. Gentry, *God Gave Wine*, Lincoln, California, Oakdown, 2001, p. 89.

10 Torah is the Hebrew word for law referring to the first five books of the Old Testament attributed to Moses. The five books are also referred to as the "Pentateuch," from the Greek language meaning five scrolls.

11 Attributed to Alexander Pope, 18th century English poet.

12 Jim West, *Drinking With Calvin And Luther*, Lincoln, California, Oakdown, 2003, p. 127.

13 Ibid., p. 128.

14 Andrew Jefford, *The Evening Standard Wine Guide 1997*, London. Andrew Jefford wrote for the Evening Standard from 1992-2002.

15 Ibid.

16 Daniel Rogov, *Rogov's Guide to Israeli Wines 2007*, London, The Toby Press, 2006, pp. 3-4.

17 Ibid., pp. 3-4.

18 Goldfisher and Sacks, *The Wine Route of Israel*, p. 11.

19 Per-Henrik Mansson and Ted Loos, "Dom Pérignon," *Wine Spectator*, October 31, 1995.

20 Cited in *West*, p. 53.

21 Cited in *West*, p. 53.

22 Cited in *West*, p. 102.

23 Cited in *West*, p. 80.

[24] Johnson, *Vintage*, p. 129.

[25] Ibid., p. 10.

[26] Jeffrey A. Miron & Jeffrey Zwiebel, "Alcohol Consumption During Prohibition," *The American Economic Review*, American Economic Association, vol. 81(2), pp. 242-247, May, 1991.

[27] Daniel Okrent, *LAST CALL: The Rise and Fall of Prohibition*, New York, Scribner, 2010.

[28] Theresa Lane, editor, *Foods That Harm Foods That Heal*, London, Readers Digest, pp. 376-377, 1996.

[29] The study was published in *Annals of Internal Medicine*, January 2, 2007, 146:10-19, and is an example of multiple studies showing wine benefits heart health.

[30] David Stipp, "Researchers Seek Key to Antiaging in Calorie Cutback," *The Wall Street Journal*, October 31, 2006.

[31] Nikoloas Scarmeas, Jose A. Luchsinger, Richard Mayeux, and Yaakov Stern, "Mediterranean diet and Alzheimer disease," *Annals of Neurology*, September 11, 2007 69:1084-1093.

[32] Cited in "Wine Drinkers May Keep Weight Off, Eat Healthier," *Wine Spectator*, May 31, 2006.

[33] Don Colbert, M.D., *What Would Jesus Eat?*, Nashville, Thomas Nelson Publishers, 2002.

[34] Harold S. Kushner, *To Life!: A Celebration of Jewish Being and Thinking*, New York, Warner Books, 1993, p. xi.

[35] Ibid., p. xi.

[36] Shane Claiborne, *Irresistible Revolution: Living As An Ordinary Radical*, Grand Rapids, Michigan, Zondervan, 2006, p.80.

[37] Conrad Gempf, *Mealtime Habits of the Messiah: 40 Encounters with Jesus*, Grand Rapids, Michigan, Zondervan, 2005, pp. 132-133.

[38] Andrea Robinson is a Master Sommelier, wine educator, and author. Two of her books are listed in Recommended Reading. Her approach is refreshing, down to earth, but very knowledgeable and great on wine and food pairings.

[39] Kevin Zraley is described as "America's ultimate wine educator." His annually published wine course is an outstanding resource for increasing your wine IQ.

[40] Robert Parker published the first issue of *The Wine Advocate* in 1978. Knowledgeable wine observers agree that *The Wine Advocate* is the most significant influence on serious wine consumers.

[41] Karen MacNeil, *The Wine Bible*, New York, Workman Publishing, 2001, p.49.

APPENDICES

Appendix 1

The chart provides a list of the Hebrew and Greek words for wine in the Bible.

In the Old Testament, the primary word for wine is *yayin*.

In the New Testament, the primary Greek word for wine is *oinos*. *Oinos* is the equivalent to the Hebrew word *yayin*. Together they are the dominant words for wine in the Bible. Both words refer to fermented beverages.

There are more words for wine in Hebrew and Greek, but are less used than *yayin* and *oinos*. The chart shows all the Hebrew and Greek words and the number of times each word is used and in how many verses. The chart will guide you into further examination of the word usage. A few verses are listed for each word for further observation and study.

Wine In Words

Hebrew Words From The Old Testament

WORD	TIMES USED IN VERSES	TRANSLATION	MEANING	REFERENCES
YAYIN	139 in 133	wine	wine, to effervesce	Numbers 28:14 Isaiah 55:1 Psalms 104:15
TIYROWSH	52 in 40	wine	sense of expulsion must of fresh juice	Deuteronomy 14:26 Isaiah 65:8 Psalms 4:7
SHEKAR	24 in 20	strong, strong wine	strong drink, alcoholic beverage, an intoxicant	Deuteronomy 14:26 Proverbs 20:1 Isaiah 28:7
YEQEB	14 in14	winepress	winepress; trough, vat	Numbers 18:27 Deuteronomy 15:14 Proverbs 3: 10
CHAMAR	11 in 11	wine	wine, troubled, foul	Ezra 7:22 Daniel 5:23 Daniel 15:1
GATH	39 in 36	winepress	winepress or vat for winepress holding grapes	Nehemiah 13:15 Joel 3:13 Judges 6:11
MAMCAK	3 in 2	wine	mixture, wine mixed with water or spices; mixed wine	Proverbs 23:30 Isaiah 65:11
COBE	6 in 5	wine	wine: drunkard (abstract-carousal, drunken)	Deuteronomy 21:20 Isaiah 1:22 Nahum 1:10
CHEMER	3 in 2	red wine	wine, as fermenting pure red wine	Deuteronomy 32:14 Isaiah 27:2
'ACIYC	7 in 5	wine; new wine	must of fresh grape juice (as just trodden out); juice, new sweet wine	Isaiah 49:26 Joel 3:18 Amos 9:13
'ENAB	20 in 18	grapes	(ripe) grape, wine	Genesis 40: 10 Numbers 6:3 Amos 9:13

Greek Words From The New Testament

WORD	TIMES USED IN VERSES	TRANSLATION	MEANING	REFERENCES
OINOS	33 in 25	wine	wine (equivalent to the primary Hebrew word YAYIN)	Matthew 9:17 Ephesians 5:18 Titus 2:3
GLEUKOS	2 in 1	wine	fermented wine	Acts 2:1 3
PAROINOS	4 in 2	wine	given to staying near wine: given to wine	I Timothy 3:3 Titus 1 :7
OINO-PHLUGIA	2 in 1	wine	excess of wine overflowing, surplus: excess of wine; drunkenness	I Peter 4:3

Appendix 2

Bible References For Wine, Vineyard, And Vine

The list of Bible references is a comprehensive listing of all verses containing the English word for wine, vine, and vineyard.

Wine

Genesis
9:21, 24
14:18
19:32, 33, 34, 35
27:25, 28, 37
49:11, 12

Exodus
29:40

Leviticus
10:9
23:13

Numbers
6:3, 20
15:5, 7, 10
18:12
28:14

Deuteronomy
7:13
11:14
12:17
14:23, 26
18:4
28:39, 51
29:6
32:33, 38

Judges
9:13
13:4, 7, 14
19:19

Ruth
2:14

1 Samuel
1:14, 15, 24
10:3
16:20
25:18

2 Samuel
13:28
16:1, 2

2 Kings
18:32

1 Chronicles
9:29
12:40
27:27

2 Chronicles
2:10, 15
11:11
31:5
32:28

Ezra
6:9
7:22

Nehemiah
2:1
5:11, 15, 18
10:37, 39
13:5, 12, 15

Esther
1:7, 8, 10
5:6
7:2, 7

Job
1:13, 18
32:19

Psalms
4:7
60:3
75:8
78:65
104:15

Proverbs
3:10
4:17
9:2, 5
20:1
21:17
23:20, 30, 31
31:4, 6

Ecclesiastes
2:3
9:7
10:19

Song of Songs
1:2, 4
4:10
5:1
7:2, 9
8:2

Isaiah
1:22
5:10, 11, 12, 22
16:10
22:13
24:7, 9, 11
25:6
28:1, 7
29:29
36:17
49:26
51:21
55:1
56:12
62:8
65:11

Jeremiah
13:12
23:9
25:15
31:12
35:2, 5, 6, 8, 14
40:10, 12
48:11, 33
51:7

Lamentations
2:12

Ezekiel
27:18
44:21

Daniel
1:5, 8, 16
5:1, 2, 4, 23
10:3

Hosea
2:8, 9, 22
4:11
7:5, 14
9:2, 4
14:7

Joel
1:5, 10
2:19, 24
3:3, 18

Amos
2:8, 12
5:11
6:6
9:13, 14

Micah
2:11
6:15

Nahum
1:10

Habakkuk
2:5

Zephaniah
1:12, 13

Haggai
1:11
2:12, 16

Zechariah
9:15, 17
10:7

Matthew
9:17
27:34, 48

Mark
2:22
15:23, 36

Luke
1:15
5:37, 38, 39
7:33
10:34
23:36

John
2:3, 9, 10
4:46
19:29

Acts
2:13

Romans
14:21

Ephesians
5:18

1 Timothy
3:8
5:23

Titus
2:3

Revelation
6:6
14:8, 10
16:19
17:2
18:3, 13

Vineyard

Genesis
9:20

Exodus
22:5
23:11

Leviticus
19:10

Numbers
20:17
21:22

Deuteronomy
20:6
22:9
23:24
24:21
28:30

1 Kings
21:1, 2, 6, 7, 15, 16, 18

Psalm
80:15

Proverbs
24:30
31:16

Song of Songs
1:6
8:11, 12

Isaiah
1:8
3:14
5:1, 3, 4, 7, 10
27:2

Jeremiah
12:10
35:7, 9

Micah
1:6
7:1

Matthew
20:1, 2, 4, 7, 8, 28,
33, 39, 40, 41

Mark
12:2, 8, 9

Luke
13:6, 7
20:9, 10, 13, 15, 16

1 Corinthians
9:7

Vine

Genesis
40:9, 10
49:11, 22

Leviticus
25:5, 11

Deuteronomy
32:32

Judges
9:12, 13

1Kings
4:25

2 Kings
4:39
18:31

Job
15:33

Psalm
80:8, 14, 16
128:3

Song of Songs
6:11
7:8

Isaiah
6:11
16:8
24:7
32:12
34:4
36:16

Jeremiah
2:21
6:9
8:13

Ezekiel
15:2, 6
17:6, 7, 8
19:10

Hosea
10:1
14:7

Joel
1:11, 12
2:22

Jonah
4:6, 7, 9, 10

Micah
4:4

Haggai
2:19

Zechariah
3:10
8:12

Malachi
3:11

Matthew
26:29

Mark
14:25

Luke	John	Revelation
22:18	5:1, 4, 5	14:18, 19

RECOMMENDED READING

Wine Education

Johnson, Hugh. 1989. *Vintage: The Story of Wine.* New York: Simon & Schuster.

Johnson, Hugh and Robinson, Jancis. 2001. *The World Atlas of Wine.* London: Mitchell Beazley.

MacNeil, Karen. 2001. *The Wine Bible.* New York. Workman Publishing.

McCarthy, Ed and Mary Ewing-Mulligan. 2006. *Wine for Dummies.* Hoboken, NJ: Wiley Publishing.

Robinson, Andrea Immer. 2005. *Great Wine Made Simple: Straight Talk from a Master Sommelier.* New York: Broadway Books.

Robinson, Jancis (ed.).1999. *The Oxford Companion To Wine.* New York: Oxford.

Zraley, Kevin. 2009. *Windows On The World Complete Wine Course.* New York: Sterling.

Spiritual

Colbert, Don, M.D. 2002. *What Would Jesus Eat?* Nashville, Tennessee: Thomas Nelson.

Gentry, Kenneth L, Jr. 2001. *God Gave Wine: What The Bible Says About Alcohol.* Lincoln, California: Oakdown.

West, Jim. 2003. *Drinking With Calvin And Luther: A History Of Alcohol In The Church*. Lincoln, California: Oakdown.

Annually Published Wine Guides

Johnson, Hugh. 2009. *Pocket Wine Book 2010*. London: Mitchell Beazley.

Parker, Robert M. Jr. 2009. *Parker's Wine Bargains: The World's Best Wine Values Under $25.00*. New York: Simon & Schuster.

Robinson, Andrea. 2009. *Andrea Robinson's 2010 Wine Buying Guide for Everyone*. Santa Barbara, California: JGR Productions.

Zraley, Kevin. 2009. *Kevin Zraley's American Wine Guide 2010*. New York: Sterling.

ABOUT THE AUTHOR

Described as a world traveler, wine aficionado, and contemporary spiritual teacher, Jerry's work and ministry has spanned thirty-five years, and has taken him to seventy countries. He served pastoral positions in churches including almost eighteen years with Willow Creek Community Church and the Willow Creek Association, where he pioneered the international ministries of each. Today, he is an independent leadership coach to pastors and ministry leaders around the world, and consults with churches and ministry organizations.

wine to water

Wine To Water is a 501(c)(3) non-profit aid organization focused on providing clean water to needy people around the world. Nearly 1 billion people in the world today lack access to adequate water and 2.5 billion people lack access to improved sanitation. We are devoted to fighting this epidemic. Wine symbolizes fortune in our society. Our goal is to give the fortunate population an opportunity to fight for those who can't fight for themselves.

Since 2004 Wine to Water has provided clean water to people in nine countries.

winetowater.org
828-355-9655
info@winetowater.org

Doc Hendley, Founder of Wine To Water, was a 2009 CNN Hero.

www.ingramcontent.com/pod-product-compliance
Lightning Source LLC
LaVergne TN
LVHW051246080426
835513LV00016B/1763